EDGAR ALLAN POE

Poems and Essays on Poetry

Edited with an introduction by
C.H. SISSON

Fyfield*Books*

CARCANET

First published in Great Britain in 1995 by
Carcanet Press Limited
Alliance House
Cross Street
Manchester M2 7AQ

This impression 2003

Selection, introduction and editorial matter © C.H. Sisson 1995, 2003

A CIP catalogue record for this book is available from the British Library
ISBN 1 85754 696 2

The publisher acknowledges financial assistance from
the Arts Council of England

Printed and bound in England by SRP Ltd, Exeter

Contents

Introduction

'Edgar Poe did not share any of those American ideas about progress, perfectability, democratic institutions and the other declared principles dear to the philistines of the two worlds.' Thus Théophile Gautier who, only two years Poe's junior, survived him by nearly a quarter of a century. Baudelaire, ten years younger than Gautier, was even more emphatic in advancing the thesis that Poe hardly fitted into his native country. 'The United States,' he said, was for him 'a vast cage, a great counting-house,' adding that 'all his life he made sinister efforts to escape the influence of this antipathetic atmosphere.' Poe was, certainly, an isolated figure, but it would be wrong to attribute that simply to the social and political conditions in the USA in the first half of the nineteenth century. It is arguable that those conditions set him some problems he would not have encountered in western Europe, as they certainly precluded some solutions which would have been available in a more close-knit and less ramshackle society. But Poe's dissatisfactions with his milieux, and his 'efforts to escape', were powered by personal peculiarities which were at once the source of his unquestionable originality and of the difficulties he encountered in exploiting it in a manner which would have both satisfied his vanity and provided him with something more recognisable as public success in his own country.

As things in fact turned out, Poe's direct influence on American, and indeed on Anglo-Saxon poetry as a whole, was small. F.O. Matthiessen makes the incontrovertible point that, 'by one of the oddest turns of literary history, Poe has been assimilated into American poetry largely through what was made of him in France.' And what was made of him in France was crucial to the evolution from Romantic to Symbolist poetry, and so, in turn, to Eliot and Stevens, to mention no others: thus, the French connection is worth some attention from the student of American poetry. Poe's name was early associated with that of possibly the greatest French poet of the nineteenth century. It may seem odd, from the point of view of the late twentieth century, that it was not the *Fleurs du mal*, but his translation of Poe's tales, which first made Charles Baudelaire famous; so at any rate Gautier, who was well placed to know, assures us. Baudelaire – to quote Gautier again – 'naturalised ... this singular genius whose individuality was so rare, so marked, so exceptional and who first scandalised, rather than charmed, America.' The translations were true to the style and thought of the original, with 'so faithful and so supple a liberty, that they produced the effect of original works.' Baudelaire did not venture to translate the poems, except for pieces quoted in tales or essays, but in his introduction to the tales he spoke of them with respect and, one might say, wonder. Gautier had no doubt about the influence of Poe on Baudelaire's own work.

It was left to Mallarmé, twenty years Baudelaire's junior, to produce a translation of the poems. Despite his own incomparable technical skill, Mallarmé did not attempt a verse translation, and had he done so he would not have pretended that French verse could reproduce the technical features of the English original. What he does claim for his version is that it tries to render 'some of the extraordinary sonorous effects of the original music and, here and there perhaps, the feeling itself'. Anyone with an ordinary reading knowledge of French will enjoy putting the two texts side by side.

If public attention in Paris went primarily to the tales, it was the application of Poe's restlessly analytical mind – so evident in the tales as well as in the writing which is specifically theoretical – to what can only be called poetics, which most profoundly influenced the work of Baudelaire, Mallarmé and Valéry. Valéry, whose mind was more consistently analytical even than Poe's, went so far as to say that Poe was 'the first to think of giving a pure theoretical basis to literary works', adding words to the effect that the attempt to cut free altogether from old ideas and to start afresh on entirely analytical bases was his own contribution. With a little of the European, and specifically French, grand manner, he says that 'this great man would be completely forgotten today, if Baudelaire had not undertaken to introduce him into European literature'. But he also underlines the importance of what Poe did:

in the midst of a people entirely busied about its material development, still indifferent to the past, organising its future

viii

and leaving the most complete liberty to experiments of all kinds, one man... was found to consider the things of the mind and, among them literary production, with a clarity, a sagacity and a lucidity which had never yet occurred, to this point, in a head endowed with poetic invention. Never before Poe had the premises of the subject been examined, reduced to a problem of psychology, and attacked by means of an analysis in which logic and the mechanics of effects were deliberately engaged.

One can hardly, without astonishment, turn from such eulogies, from the summits of literary intellectuality in Paris, to the actual conditions of Poe's origins and education, or indeed to the course of his public literary life. He was born in Boston in 1809. No great reliance is to be placed on his own statements about his family and upbringing, and it must be said that, at various times of his life, he exhibited a less than average addiction to the truth. The facts seem to be that his parents were both actors – his mother, at least, one of some talent. She died before he was three years old; his father seems to have disappeared shortly before that date. Edgar was the second of three children. After the death of their mother Edgar was looked after – but never adopted – by John and Frances Allan, who lived in Richmond, Virginia. Allan was a tobacco exporter and general merchant, well off, certainly, by any standard to which the Poe family were accustomed. When Edgar was six, the Allan family went to England on an extended business trip. They took the boy with them, and for five years he had an English education, latterly at a school in North London. There he was known by the name of Allan, but, on returning to Richmond, he reverted to that of Poe – possibly a sign that John Allan was distancing himself from him. However that may be, in 1826 he was sent to the University of Virginia. That lasted only a year: he found himself among rich young men and appears to have been determined not to be out-done at card-playing and drinking; he ran up debts which Allan declined to pay. In March, 1827, he left the Allans' house, in his own words 'to find a place in the wide world' where he would not be treated as Allan had treated him. He went off by ship to Boston, where he joined the army, but not before he had arranged for the printing of forty copies of a book of his poems – presumably as a visiting card rather than in the hope of making a fortune. When Frances Allan died in February, 1829, John Allan not only bought Edgar a suit of black clothes but supported his release from the ranks of the army and his re-enlistment as a cadet at West Point. This did not last: Poe deliberately forced the authorities to expel him. Early in 1831 he was in New York, and published a revised and expanded edition of his poems.

The turbulence of Poe's life makes it wholly understandable that his anchorage with John Allan became insecure – and Poe needed an anchorage. In Baltimore he found one of great steadiness with his aunt, Maria Clemm, a widow with a small child, Virginia, whom Poe married some seven years after their first meeting, by which time she was thirteen; he was twenty-seven. The story of Poe's life, from the time of his expulsion from West Point, is largely one of trying, with varying degrees of success and unsuccess, to make a living by writing and editing. Julian Symons, in his excellent biography, speaks of his 'constant struggle for money, the pride and the drinking, the extent to which criticism and fiction were his occupation although poetry was his ideal'. Of the numerous newspapers and magazines with which he was at one time or another connected, none corresponded with his notion of what such a journal should be, and although one can readily believe that he was not the easiest of colleagues, one cannot but have a profound sympathy for his passionate desire, which the years only increased, to have a magazine of his own which would be a proper vehicle for what he had to offer.

There is no question of Poe not being able to publish what he wrote; his prose output, in a writing life of little over twenty years, is remarkable for its variety and its originality. The tales alone would have given him a place among the most innovative writers of the century; the critical writings – of varying quality but all bearing the stamp of a mind of outstanding analytical capacity, if also of a certain impatience and a certain arrogance – included some which had in them the seeds of literary developments certainly unguessed at by their first readers. It was not for lack of elbowing his way that Poe failed to achieve his ambition of controlling a paper of unquestionable literary significance. All this activity did not still his lifelong ambition not merely to be, but to be recognised as being, primarily a poet. At the beginning of his literary career, when sending a proof of his poems to an influential critic – no doubt in the by no means exceptional hope that he was about to be made famous – he wrote:

> I am young – not yet twenty – *am* a poet – if deep worship of all beauty can make me one – and wish to be so in the common meaning of the word. I would give the world to embody half the ideas afloat in my imagination.

Such sentiments are not unusual; the unusual element, in Poe's case, is that, even at this time, he had actually written poems – notably the first 'To Helen' (p.1) – which justified his claims. What all his efforts failed to make clear to his contemporaries was that being a poet entitled him to financial support – a romantic notion which persists among the ignorant young and among some who should know better. Baudelaire himself, in his notes on Poe, asks the question: 'Is there a diabolical Providence which prepares misfortune from the cradle?' He goes on to cite other cases – even that of Vauvenargues, whose works are instinct with an experience which only the ordinary world could have given him, and whom Baudelaire pities for being left to 'grow his sickly leaves in the coarse atmosphere of a barracks' – following a career which could almost be taken for granted in one of the minor nobility. If the buffetings of Poe's career as a journalist did not allow him the freedom to which he thought himself entitled, the theory of poetry he developed in this milieu corresponded perfectly with the aspirations he had expressed as a young man 'not yet twenty'.

These ideas are set out in the essays on poetry contained in this small volume. Baudelaire summarised the drift of them as: 'the principle of poetry is, strictly and simply, human aspiration towards a higher beauty.' The language sounds odd, today, but it corresponds almost precisely with Poe's definition, in 'The Poetic Principle' (p.88), of 'the Poetry of Words as *The Rhythmical Creation of Beauty*'. The omission of 'rhythmical' in Baudelaire's formulation marks an emphasis which changes its character as the poems of Poe passed from America to the European mainland, from native English-speakers to those to whom English was a foreign language. The rhythms of ordinary conversations, whether in America or England, are markedly different from those of the French, and the way the language falls has resulted, over the centuries, in radically different practices in versification. It would be possible to exaggerate the extent to which this has contributed to the relatively high rating given to Poe's poetry in France, as compared with English-speaking countries, but a French reader might well be less shocked than an American or an Englishman by what F.O. Matthiessen calls 'one or two notorious stunts like "The Bells", which no adult reader can now face without pain'. Such stunts, however, do nothing to invalidate Poe's poetical doctrine. 'I hold that a long poem does not exist,' Poe says, '...a poem deserves its title only inasmuch as it excites, by elevating the soul...But all excitements are, through a psychal necessity, transient. That degree of excitement which would entitle a poem to be so called at all, cannot be sustained throughout a composition of any great length.' So *Paradise Lost* is to be regarded as poetical only when...we view it merely as a series of minor poems' – 'minor' meaning, in Poe's terminology, 'of little length'. This did not prevent him describing his 'Eureka', an essay of a hundred pages on the little matter of 'The Material and Spiritual Universe', as 'A Prose Poem', adding in the preface: 'it is as a Poem that I wish this work to be judged after I am dead.'

The second pillar of Poe's theory of poetry is his hostility to 'the heresy of *The Didactic*. It has been assumed,' he says, '...that the ultimate object of all Poetry is Truth...With as deep a reverence for the True as ever inspired the bosom of man,' he goes on (rather over-boldly, one may think, however little one knows of the confusions of Poe's life), 'I would nevertheless limit, in some measure, its modes of inculcation' – in order, apparently, not to enfeeble them. 'The demands of Truth are severe.' He proceeds to chop 'the world of mind' into three parts, and to assign Truth to Intellect, Beauty to Taste, and Duty to Moral Sense. This implausible piece of dogmatism survives in Valéry in the guise of a plea that the modern tendency is to separate manners and fields of activity more clearly than ever before, so that each can realise its function more fully and occur 'in a pure state'. Poetic pleasure is itself 'absolute poetry'. Well, maybe, and certainly pleasure need not be as impure as it often is, but perhaps 'the real language of men' still has a part to play in it.

Valéry's claim was that Poe was the first to give a pure theoretical basis to literary works might be said to be made good by 'The Philosophy of Composition', if one could take that remarkable production wholly seriously, as Valéry probably could. The essay is an analysis of 'The Raven', undertaken, according to its author, with the 'design to render it manifest that no one point in its composition is referable either to accident or intuition – that the work proceeded step by step, to its completion, with the precision and rigid consequence of a mathematical problem.' The analysis itself is a *tour de force* of deliberation, of a kind which could not fail to impress Valéry, however incredible it may be to lesser mortals, as an account of how a poem could be written. Poe starts with the consideration of 'extent', and finds the proper length to be about one hundred lines. He goes on to the choice of an 'impression to be given' by the poem and to such matters as settling what the refrain shall be. Mallarmé tells how Mme Suzan Achard Wirds was assured by Poe that

> the story published by him of the method of composition [of 'The Raven'] had absolutely no authenticity; and that he had not expected that people would think that it had. The idea came to him, suggested by the commentaries and investigations of critics, that the poem could have been composed in that way...it had amused and surprised him to see it so promptly accepted as a declaration made *bone fide*.

Certainly Poe's theories about poetry, interesting though they are and influential though they have been, are less to be taken to heart than the poems themselves. Whatever one's view of the status of *la poésie pure* – and it is probably best understood as pointing to an essential element in poetry rather than as an exclusive definition – there is a small handful of Poe's poems which are of a clarity and luminosity which make most of the poetry of the nineteenth century look muddy. These poems demand the kind of attention which his definition of the 'Poetry of Words' demands;

no less, but, equally certainly, no more. To brood on such questions as the degree of sexual involvement – usually thought to be slight – with whoever among his acquaintance was for the time being serving as his model of the feminine ideal, may be a more or less innocent amusement, but it has nothing to do with reading the poems. 'The Rhythmical Creation of Beauty' excludes all notions of truth, all questions of correspondence of word with fact – a high-handed demand to make, not only on any research worker, but on any ordinary reader. Yet it is this exclusion that is called for by the notion of pure poetry of which he was the first and most dramatic exponent.

The early poem which stands first in this volume, as it did in 'The Raven, and Other Poems', as revised by Poe himself for the American edition of 1845, begins 'Helen, thy beauty is to me / Like that Nicean bark of yore . . .'. It is pure poetry as Poe conceived it. The meaning does not matter, and it should be read simply for the pleasure it can give, however incorrect that advice must seem to the *aficionado* of explanations. Surrendering oneself to the pleasure is itself a discipline, and the reader who is incapable of it is insensitive to poetry, or at any rate to the essentials of it below the sometimes important accidents which may accompany them. 'The Valley of Unrest' can, likewise, raise psychological/biographical questions which may conceivably be worth exploring, but they should not be allowed to interfere with what might be described as the helpless reading of the poem. A certain mysterious charm survives even in the prose of Mallarmé's translations, so that one cannot dismiss the contents as having no part in the poetic effects, but the sound and fall of the verse, once heard, cannot be separated from them. 'The Valley of Unrest' is by no means the strongest of Poe's exercises with a form of couplet: the masterpieces are undoubtedly 'The Sleeper' and 'The City in the Sea', yet both these are so slight as at times to verge on absurdity:

> Where the people did not dwell;
> They had gone unto the wars,
> Trusting to the mild-eyed stars

– or even the in their kind stunning lines: 'Resignedly beneath the sky / The melancholy waters lie.'

In spite of the many explications in which Poe, at one time or another, revelled, it would hardly be in disaccord with the core of his doctrine to say that pure poetry is, as to its essential nature, enjoyable but not explicable, though this leaves plenty of work for critics among the inessential elements which can, in any case, contribute to the real pleasure which poems may give through their accidental features. No use looking, in Poe, for the moral and prophetic force of Milton's sonnets, the insight and grasp of reality of Marvell's 'Horatian Ode', or Wordsworth's sense of the natural world, or indeed for many of the major or minor features which give the works of other poets much of their interest. The critic may seek to discredit 'The Bells' or 'The Raven' for the crude ingenuity of their structure and rhythms but, in the handful of poems in which there is no touch of grotesqueness, Poe succeeds in 'the rhythmical creation of beauty' in a manner which the occasional excesses in a handful of others merely emphasise. The sceptic should perhaps start with the seventy or so lines of the second, later, poem 'To Helen' (p.73). There is no distraction by noisy or emphatic elements of rhyme or rhythm, and the poem is not so much to be read as to be breathed: 'Upon the upturn'd faces of a thousand / Roses that grew in that enchanted garden.' The same goes for 'To ----': 'Not long ago, the writer of these lines, / In the mad pride of intellectuality,' which at least seems to hesitate on the threshold of ordinary human speech, and may be recommended as an introduction to those who, entangled in the tastes and prejudices of twentieth-century 'self-expression', may hanker for at least some touch of the living world.

Those who prefer dark ladies to sonnets – and they are many – may like to root among the accounts of Poe's last years to sort out the confusions of his relationships – all, it may be assumed, unconsummated, but involving more than one proposal of marriage – with Sarah Whitman, Annie Richmond, and Elmira Shelton. A letter of October, 1848, almost exactly a year before his death, claims that when he spoke to the first of these ladies he 'loved for the first time', and it goes on to ask:

Do you not feel in your inmost heart of hearts that the 'Soul-love' of which the world speaks so often and so idly is, in this

xv

instance at least, but the veriest, the most absolute of realities? Do you not perceive that it is my diviner nature – my spiritual being – which burns and pants to commingle with your own?

The marriage with Sarah Whitman not taking place, there was still time for more or less wild grabs in the direction of Annie Richmond and Elmira Shelton, the latter apparently a childhood sweet-heart. But there is little doubt that the agonies of Poe's last days were financial as much as amorous, and that he was appalled by his relative lack of success as a writer. It was in Baltimore that he was picked up on the street, unconcious – and if he was drunk, that was certainly not the only thing that was the matter with him. He died four days later, on 7 October, 1849.

A Note on Punctuation

Poe's punctuation – particularly his fondness for the parenthetical dash and his treatment of quotations – often looks odd to the modern reader. Where this seems integral to the character and texture of his writing, it has been left unaltered; however, there are a number of other places, chiefly in the essays, where the original punctuation might seem confusing or simply incorrect, and here it has been silently brought into line with modern usage. Most of these instances involved the transfer of an intrusive semi-colon or full-stop at the end of a quotation from within the quotation-marks to outside them; similarly-placed commas have been moved only if they would otherwise look distractingly wrong.

POEMS

To Helen

Helen, thy beauty is to me
  Like those Nicéan barks of yore,
That gently, o'er a perfumed sea,
  The weary, wayworn wanderer bore
  To his own native shore.

On desperate seas long wont to roam,
  Thy hyacinth hair, thy classic face,
Thy Naiad airs have brought me home
  To the glory that was Greece,
  And the grandeur that was Rome.

Lo! in yon brilliant window niche
  How statue-like I see thee stand,
  The agate lamp within thy hand!
Ah, Psyche, from the regions which
  Are Holy Land!

The Raven

Once upon a midnight dreary, while I pondered, weak and weary,
Over many a quaint and curious volume of forgotten lore,
While I nodded, nearly napping, suddenly there came a tapping,
As of some one gently rapping, rapping at my chamber door.
''Tis some visiter,' I muttered, 'tapping at my chamber door –
      Only this, and nothing more.'

1

Ah, distinctly I remember it was in the bleak December,
And each separate dying ember wrought its ghost upon the floor.
Eagerly I wished the morrow; – vainly I had sought to borrow
From my books surcease of sorrow – sorrow for the lost Lenore –
For the rare and radiant maiden whom the angels name Lenore –
Nameless here for evermore.

And the silken sad uncertain rustling of each purple curtain
Thrilled me – filled me with fantastic terrors never felt before;
So that now, to still the beating of my heart, I stood repeating
''Tis some visiter entreating entrance at my chamber door –
Some late visiter entreating entrance at my chamber door; –
This it is, and nothing more.'

Presently my soul grew stronger; hesitating then no longer,
'Sir,' said I, 'or Madam, truly your forgiveness I implore;
But the fact is I was napping, and so gently you came rapping,
And so faintly you came tapping, tapping at my chamber door,
That I scarce was sure I heard you' – here I opened wide the door; –
Darkness there, and nothing more.

Deep into that darkness peering, long I stood there wondering,
fearing,
Doubting, dreaming dreams no mortal ever dared to dream before;
But the silence was unbroken, and the darkness gave no token,
And the only word there spoken was the whispered word,
'Lenore!'
This I whispered, and an echo murmured back the word, 'Lenore!'
Merely this and nothing more.

Back into the chamber turning, all my soul within me burning,
Soon again I heard a tapping somewhat louder than before.
'Surely,' said I, 'surely that is something at my window lattice;
Let me see, then, what thereat is, and this mystery explore –
Let my heart be still a moment and this mystery explore; –
'Tis the wind and nothing more!'

Open here I flung the shutter, when, with many a flirt and flutter,
In there stepped a stately raven of the saintly days of yore.
Not the least obeisance made he; not an instant stopped or stayed
     he;
But, with mien of lord or lady, perched above my chamber door –
Perched upon a bust of Pallas just above my chamber door –
               Perched, and sat, and nothing more.

Then this ebony bird beguiling my sad fancy into smiling,
By the grave and stern decorum of the countenance it wore,
'Though thy crest be shorn and shaven, thou,' I said, 'art sure no
     craven,
Ghastly grim and ancient raven wandering from the Nightly
     shore –
Tell me what thy lordly name is on the Night's Plutonian shore!'
               Quoth the raven, 'Nevermore.'

Much I marvelled this ungainly fowl to hear discourse so plainly,
Though its answer little meaning – little relevancy bore;
For we cannot help agreeing that no living human being
Ever yet was blessed with seeing bird above his chamber door –
Bird or beast upon the sculptured bust above his chamber door,
               With such name as 'Nevermore.'

But the raven, sitting lonely on the placid bust, spoke only
That one word, as if his soul in that one word he did outpour.
Nothing further then he uttered – not a feather then he fluttered –
Till I scarcely more than muttered, 'Other friends have flown
     before –
On the morrow *he* will leave me, as my hopes have flown before.'
               Then the bird said, 'Nevermore.'

Startled at the stillness broken by reply so aptly spoken,
'Doubtless,' said I, 'what it utters is its only stock and store,
Caught from some unhappy master whom unmerciful Disaster
Followed fast and followed faster till his songs one burden bore –
Till the dirges of his Hope that melancholy burden bore
               Of "Never – nevermore."'

3

But the raven still beguiling all my sad soul into smiling,
Straight I wheeled a cushioned seat in front of bird and bust and
     door;
Then, upon the velvet sinking, I betook myself to linking
Fancy unto fancy, thinking what this ominous bird of yore –
What this grim, ungainly, ghastly, gaunt, and ominous bird of yore
            Meant in croaking 'Nevermore.'

This I sat engaged in guessing, but no syllable expressing
To the fowl whose fiery eyes now burned into my bosom's core;
This and more I sat divining, with my head at ease reclining
On the cushion's velvet lining that the lamp-light gloated o'er,
But whose velvet violet lining with the lamp-light gloating o'er,
            She shall press, ah, nevermore!

Then, methought, the air grew denser, perfumed from an unseen
     censer
Swung by angels whose faint foot-falls tinkled on the tufted floor.
'Wretch,' I cried, 'thy God hath lent thee – by these angels he hath
     sent thee
Respite – respite and nepenthe from thy memories of Lenore!
Quaff, oh quaff this kind nepenthe, and forget this lost Lenore!'
            Quoth the raven, 'Nevermore.'

'Prophet!' said I, 'thing of evil! – prophet still, if bird or devil! –
Whether Tempter sent, or whether tempest tossed thee here
     ashore,
Desolate yet all undaunted, on this desert land enchanted –
On this home by Horror haunted – tell me truly, I implore –
Is there – *is* there balm in Gilead? – tell me – tell me, I implore!'
            Quoth the raven, 'Nevermore.'

'Prophet!' said I, 'thing of evil – prophet still, if bird or devil!
By that Heaven that bends above us – by that God we both adore –
Tell this soul with sorrow laden if, within the distant Aidenn,
It shall clasp a sainted maiden whom the angels name Lenore –
Clasp a rare and radiant maiden whom the angels name Lenore?'
            Quoth the raven, 'Nevermore.'

'Be that word our sign of parting, bird or fiend!' I shrieked,
    upstarting –
'Get thee back into the tempest and the Night's Plutonian shore!
Leave no black plume as a token of that lie thy soul hath spoken!
Leave my loneliness unbroken! – quit the bust above my door!
Take thy beak from out my heart, and take thy form from off my
    door!'
                    Quoth the raven, 'Nevermore.'

And the raven, never flitting, still is sitting, still is sitting
On the pallid bust of Pallas just above my chamber door;
And his eyes have all the seeming of a demon's that is dreaming,
And the lamp-light o'er him streaming throws his shadow on the
    floor;
And my soul from out that shadow that lies floating on the floor
                    Shall be lifted – nevermore!

The Valley of Unrest

Once it smiled a silent dell
Where the people did not dwell;
They had gone unto the wars,
Trusting to the mild-eyed stars,
Nightly, from their azure towers,
To keep watch above the flowers,
In the midst of which all day
The red sun-light lazily lay.
Now each visiter shall confess
The sad valley's restlessness.
Nothing there is motionless –
Nothing save the airs that brood
Over the magic solitude.
Ah, by no wind are stirred those trees
That palpitate like the chill seas

5

Around the misty Hebrides!
Ah, by no wind those clouds are driven
That rustle through the unquiet Heaven
Uneasily, from morn till even,
Over the violets there that lie
In myriad types of the human eye –
Over the lilies there that wave
And weep above a nameless grave!
They wave: – from out their fragrant tops
Eternal dews come down in drops.
They weep: – from off their delicate stems
Perennial tears descend in gems.

Bridal Ballad

The ring is on my hand,
    And the wreath is on my brow;
Satins and jewels grand
Are all at my command,
    And I am happy now.

And my lord he loves me well;
    But, when first he breathed his vow,
I felt my bosom swell –
For the words rang as a knell,
And the voice seemed *his* who fell
In the battle down the dell,
    And who is happy now.

But he spoke to reassure me,
    And he kissed my pallid brow,
While a reverie came o'er me,
And to the churchyard bore me,
And I sighed to him before me,
Thinking him dead D'Elormie,
    'Oh, I am happy now!'

And thus the words were spoken,
    And this the plighted vow,
And, though my faith be broken,
And, though my heart be broken,
Behind the golden token
    That *proves* me happy now!

Would God I could awaken!
    For I dream I know not how,
And my soul is sorely shaken
Lest an evil step be taken, –
Lest the dead who is forsaken
    May not be happy now.

The Sleeper

At midnight, in the month of June,
I stand beneath the mystic moon.
An opiate vapor, dewy, dim,
Exhales from out her golden rim,
And, softly dripping, drop by drop,
Upon the quiet mountain top,
Steals drowsily and musically
Into the universal valley.
The rosemary nods upon the grave;
The lily lolls upon the wave;
Wrapping the fog about its breast,
The ruin moulders into rest;
Looking like Lethe, see! the lake
A conscious slumber seems to take,
And would not, for the world, awake.
All Beauty sleeps! – and lo! where lies
(Her casement open to the skies)
Irene, with her Destinies!

Oh, lady bright! can it be right –
This window open to the night?
The wanton airs, from the tree-top,
Laughingly through the lattice drop –
The bodiless airs, a wizard rout,
Flit through thy chamber in and out,
And wave the curtain canopy
So fitfully – so fearfully –
Above the closed and fringed lid
'Neath which thy slumb'ring soul lies hid,
That, o'er the floor and down the wall,
Like ghosts the shadows rise and fall!
Oh, lady dear, hast thou no fear?
Why and what art thou dreaming here?
Sure thou art come o'er far-off seas,
A wonder to these garden trees!
Strange is thy pallor! strange thy dress!
Strange, above all, thy length of tress,
And this all-solemn silentness!

The lady sleeps! Oh, may her sleep,
Which is enduring, so be deep!
Heaven have her in its sacred keep!
This chamber changed for one more holy,
This bed for one more melancholy,
I pray to God that she may lie
Forever with unopened eye,
While the dim sheeted ghosts go by!

My love, she sleeps! Oh, may her sleep,
As it is lasting, so be deep!
Soft may the worms about her creep!
Far in the forest, dim and old,
For her may some tall vault unfold –
Some vault that oft hath flung its black
And winged panels fluttering back,
Triumphant, o'er the crested palls,
Of her grand family funerals –

Some sepulchre, remote, alone,
Against whose portal she hath thrown
In childhood many an idle stone –
Some tomb from out whose sounding door
She ne'er shall force an echo more,
Thrilling to think, poor child of sin!
It was the dead who groaned within.

The Coliseum

Type of the antique Rome! Rich reliquary
Of lofty contemplation left to Time
By buried centuries of pomp and power!
At length – at length – after so many days
Of weary pilgrimage and burning thirst
(Thirst for the springs of lore that in thee lie),
I kneel, an altered and an humble man,
Amid thy shadows, and so drink within
My very soul thy grandeur, gloom, and glory!

Vastness! and Age! and Memories of Eld!
Silence! and Desolation! and dim Night!
I feel ye now – I feel ye in your strength –
O spells more sure than e'er Judæan king
Taught in the gardens of Gethsemane!
O charms more potent than the rapt Chaldee
Ever drew down from out the quiet stars!

Here, where a hero fell, a column falls!
Here, where the mimic eagle glared in gold,
A midnight vigil holds the swarthy bat!
Here, where the dames of Rome their gilded hair
Waved to the wind, now wave the reed and thistle!
Here, where on golden throne the monarch lolled,

9

Glides, spectre-like, unto his marble home,
Lit by the wan light of the hornéd moon,
The swift and silent lizard of the stones!

But stay! these walls – these ivy-clad arcades –
These mouldering plinths – these sad and blackened shafts –
These vague entablatures – this crumbling frieze –
These shattered cornices – this wreck – this ruin –
These stones – alas! these grey stones – are they all –
All of the famed, and the colossal left
By the corrosive Hours to Fate and me?

'Not all' – the Echoes answer me – 'not all!
Prophetic sounds and loud, arise forever
From us, and from all Ruin, unto the wise,
As melody from Memnon to the Sun.
We rule the hearts of mightiest men – we rule
With a despotic sway all giant minds.
We are not impotent – we pallid stones.
Not all our power is gone – not all our fame –
Not all the magic of our high renown –
Not all the wonder that encircles us –
Not all the mysteries that in us lie –
Not all the memories that hang upon
And cling around about us as a garment,
Clothing us in a robe of more than glory.'

Lenore

Ah, broken is the golden bowl! the spirit flown forever!
Let the bell toll! – a saintly soul floats on the Stygian river;
And, Guy de Vere, hast *thou* no tear? – weep now or never more!
See! on yon drear and rigid bier low lies thy love, Lenore!
Come! let the burial rite be read – the funeral song be sung! –
An anthem for the queenliest dead that ever died so young –
A dirge for her the doubly dead in that she died so young.

'Wretches! ye loved her for her wealth and hated her for her
    pride,
And when she fell in feeble health, ye blessed her – that she died!
How *shall* the ritual, then, be read? – the requiem how be sung
By you – by yours, the evil eye, – by yours, the slanderous tongue
That did to death the innocent that died, and died so young?'

Peccavimus; but rave not thus! and let a Sabbath song
Go up to God so solemnly the dead may feel no wrong!
The sweet Lenore hath 'gone before,' with Hope, that flew
    beside,
Leaving thee wild for the dear child that should have been thy
    bride –
For her, the fair and *debonair*, that now so lowly lies,
The life upon her yellow hair but not within her eyes –
The life still there, upon her hair – the death upon her eyes.

'Avaunt! to-night my heart is light. No dirge will I upraise,
But waft the angel on her flight with a Påan of old days!
Let *no* bell toll! – lest her sweet soul, amid its hallowed mirth,
Should catch the note, as it doth float – up from the damnéd
    Earth.
To friends above, from fiends below, the indignant ghost is
    riven –
From Hell unto a high estate far up within the Heaven –
From grief and groan, to a golden throne, beside the King of
    Heaven.'

Catholic Hymn

    At morn – at noon – at twilight dim –
    Maria! thou hast heard my hymn!
    In joy and wo – in good and ill –
    Mother of God, be with me still!
    When the Hours flew brightly by,

And not a cloud obscured the sky,
My soul, lest it should truant be,
Thy grace did guide to thine and thee;
Now, when storms of Fate o'ercast
Darkly my Present and my Past,
Let my Future radiant shine
With sweet hopes of thee and thine!

Israfel[1]

In Heaven a spirit doth dwell
   'Whose heart-strings are a lute;'
None sing so wildly well
As the angel Israfel,
And the giddy tears (so legends tell),
Ceasing their hymns, attend the spell
   Of his voice, all mute.

Tottering above
   In her highest noon,
   The enamored moon
Blushes with love,
   While, to listen, the red levin
   (With the rapid Pleiads, even,
   Which were seven),
   Pauses in heaven.

And they say (the starry choir
   And the other listening things)
That Israfeli's fire
Is owing to that lyre
   By which he sits and sings –
The trembling living wire
   Of those unusual strings.

[1] And the angel Israfel, whose heart-strings are a lute, and who has the sweetest voice of all God's creatures. – *Koran*.

But the skies that angel trod,
    Where deep thoughts are a duty –
Where Love's a grown-up God –
    Where the Houri glances are
Imbued with all the beauty
    Which we worship in a star.

Therefore, thou art not wrong,
    Israfeli, who despisest
An unimpassioned song;
To thee the laurels belong,
    Best bard, because the wisest!
Merrily live and long!

The ecstasies above
    With thy burning measures suit –
Thy grief, thy joy, thy hate, thy love,
    With the fervor of thy lute –
    Well may the stars be mute!

Yes, Heaven is thine; but this
    Is a world of sweets and sours;
    Our flowers are merely – flowers,
And the shadow of thy perfect bliss
    Is the sunshine of ours.

If I could dwell
Where Israfel
    Hath dwelt, and he where I,
He might not sing so wildly well
    A mortal melody,
While a bolder note than this might swell
    From my lyre within the sky.

Dreamland

By a route obscure and lonely,
Haunted by ill angels only,
Where an Eidolon, named NIGHT,
On a black throne reigns upright,
I have reached these lands but newly
From an ultimate dim Thule –
From a wild weird clime that lieth, sublime,
   Out of SPACE – out of TIME.

Bottomless vales and boundless floods,
And chasms, and caves, and Titan woods,
With forms that no man can discover
For the dews that drip all over;
Mountains toppling evermore
Into seas without a shore;
Seas that restlessly aspire,
Surging, unto skies of fire;
Lakes that endlessly outspread
Their lone waters – lone and dead, –
Their still waters – still and chilly
With the snows of the lolling lily.

By the lakes that thus outspread
Their lone waters, lone and dead, –
Their sad waters, sad and chilly
With the snows of the lolling lily, –
By the mountains – near the river
Murmuring lowly, murmuring ever, –
By the grey woods, – by the swamp
Where the toad and the newt encamp, –
By the dismal tarns and pools
   Where dwell the Ghouls, –
By each spot the most unholy –
In each nook most melancholy, –
There the traveller meets aghast
Sheeted Memories of the Past –

Shrouded forms that start and sigh
As they pass the wanderer by –
White-robed forms of friends long given,
In agony, to the Earth – and Heaven.

For the heart whose woes are legion
'Tis a peaceful, soothing region –
For the spirit that walks in shadow
'Tis – oh, 'tis an Eldorado!
But the traveller, travelling through it,
May not – dare not openly view it;
Never its mysteries are exposed
To the weak human eye unclosed;
So wills its king, who hath forbid
The uplifting of the fringed lid;
And thus the sad Soul that here passes
Beholds it but through darkened glasses.

By a route obscure and lonely,
Haunted by ill angels only,
Where an Eidolon, named NIGHT,
On a black throne reigns upright,
I have wandered home but newly
From this ultimate dim Thule.

Sonnet: To Zante

Fair isle, that from the fairest of all flowers,
    Thy gentlest of all gentle names dost take!
How many memories of what radiant hours
    At sight of thee and thine at once awake!
How many scenes of what departed bliss!
    How many thoughts of what entombéd hopes!
How many visions of a maiden that is
    No more – no more upon thy verdant slopes!

No more! alas, that magical sad sound
   Transforming all! Thy charm shall please *no more* –
Thy memory *no more!* Accurséd ground!
   Henceforth I hold thy flower-enamelled shore,
O hyacinthine isle! O purple Zante!
   'Isola d'oro! Fior di Levante!'

The City in the Sea

Lo! Death has reared himself a throne
In a strange city lying alone
Far down within the dim West,
Where the good and the bad and the worst and the best,
Have gone to their eternal rest.
Their shrines and palaces and towers
(Time-eaten towers that tremble not!)
Resemble nothing that is ours.
Around, by lifting winds forgot,
Resignedly beneath the sky
The melancholy waters lie.

No rays from the holy heaven come down
On the long night-time of that town;
But light from out the lurid sea
Streams up the turrets silently –
Gleams up the pinnacles far and free –
Up domes – up spires – up kingly halls –
Up fanes – up Babylon-like walls –
Up shadowy long-forgotten bowers
Of sculptured ivy and stone flowers –
Up many and many a marvellous shrine
Whose wreathéd friezes intertwine
The viol, the violet, and the vine.

Resignedly beneath the sky
The melancholy waters lie.
So blend the turrets and shadows there
That all seem pendulous in air,
While from a proud tower in the town
Death looks gigantically down.

There open fanes and gaping graves
Yawn level with the luminous waves;
But not the riches there that lie
In each idol's diamond eye –
Not the gaily-jewelled dead
Tempt the waters from their bed;
For no ripples curl, alas!
Along that wilderness of glass –
No swellings tell that winds may be
Upon some far-off happier sea –
No heavings hint that winds have been
On seas less hideously serene.

But lo, a stir is in the air!
The wave – there is a movement there!
As if the towers had thrust aside,
In slightly sinking, the dull tide –
As if their tops had feebly given
A void within the filmy Heaven.
The waves have now a redder glow –
The hours are breathing faint and low –
And when, amid no earthly moans,
Down, down that town shall settle hence,
Hell, rising from a thousand thrones,
Shall do it reverence.

To One in Paradise

Thou wast all that to me, love,
  For which my soul did pine –
A green isle in the sea, love,
  A fountain and a shrine,
All wreathed with fairy fruits and flowers,
  And all the flowers were mine.

Ah, dream too bright to last!
  Ah, starry Hope! that didst arise
But to be overcast!
  A voice from out the Future cries,
'On! on!' – but o'er the Past
  (Dim gulf!) my spirit hovering lies
Mute, motionless, aghast!

For, alas! alas! with me
  The light of Life is o'er!
  No more – no more – no more –
(Such language holds the solemn sea
  To the sands upon the shore)
Shall bloom the thunder-blasted tree,
  Or the stricken eagle soar!

And all my days are trances,
  And all my nightly dreams
Are where thy dark eye glances,
  And where thy footstep gleams –
In what ethereal dances,
  By what eternal streams.

Eulalie

I dwelt alone
In a world of moan,
And my soul was a stagnant tide,
Till the fair and gentle Eulalie became my blushing bride –
Till the yellow-haired young Eulalie became my smiling bride.

Ah, less – less bright
The stars of the night
Than the eyes of the radiant girl!
And never a flake
That the vapor can make
With the moon-tints of purple and pearl,
Can vie with the modest Eulalie's most unregarded curl –
Can compare with the bright-eyed Eulalie's most humble and
    careless curl.

Now Doubt – now Pain
Come never again,
For her soul gives me sigh for sigh,
And all day long
Shines, bright and strong,
Astarté within the sky,
While ever to her dear Eulalie upturns her matron eye –
While ever to her young Eulalie upturns her violet eye.

To F——s S. O——d

Thou wouldst be loved? – then let thy heart
    From its present pathway part not!
Being everything which now thou art,
    Be nothing which thou art not.
So with the world thy gentle ways,
    Thy grace, thy more than beauty,
Shall be an endless theme of praise,
    And love – a simple duty.

To F——

Beloved! amid the earnest woes
    That crowd around my earthly path –
(Drear path, alas! where grows
Not even one lonely rose) –
    My soul at least a solace hath
In dreams of thee, and therein knows
An Eden of bland repose.

And thus thy memory is to me
    Like some enchanted far-off isle
In some tumultuous sea –
Some ocean throbbing far and free
    With storms – but where meanwhile
Serenest skies continually
    Just o'er that one bright island smile.

Sonnet: Silence

There are some qualities – some incorporate things,
    That have a double life, which thus is made
A type of that twin entity which springs
    From matter and light, evinced in solid and shade.
There is a twofold *Silence* – sea and shore –
    Body and soul. One dwells in lonely places,
    Newly with grass o'ergrown; some solemn graces,
Some human memories and tearful lore,
Render him terrorless: his name's 'No More.'
He is the corporate Silence: dread him not!
    No power hath he of evil in himself;
But should some urgent fate (untimely lot!)
    Bring thee to meet his shadow (nameless elf,
That haunteth the lone regions where hath trod
No foot of man), commend thyself to God!

The Conqueror Worm

Lo! 'tis a gala night
　　Within the lonesome latter years!
An angel throng, bewinged, bedight
　　In veils, and drowned in tears,
Sit in a theatre, to see
　　A play of hopes and fears,
While the orchestra breathes fitfully
　　The music of the spheres.

Mimes, in the form of God on high,
　　Mutter and mumble low,
And hither and thither fly –
　　Mere puppets they, who come and go
At bidding of vast formless things
　　That shift the scenery to and fro,
Flapping from out their Condor wings
　　Invisible Wo!

That motley drama – oh, be sure
　　It shall not be forgot!
With its Phantom chased for evermore
　　By a crowd that seize it not,
Through a circle that ever returneth in
　　To the self-same spot,
And much of Madness, and more of Sin,
　　And Horror the soul of the plot.

But see, amid the mimic rout
　　A crawling shape intrude!
A blood-red thing that writhes from out
　　The scenic solitude!
It writhes! – it writhes! – with mortal pangs
　　The mimes become its food,
And the seraphs sob at vermin fangs
　　In human gore imbued.

Out – out are the lights – out all!
   And, over each quivering form,
The curtain, a funeral pall,
   Comes down with the rush of a storm,
And the angels, all pallid and wan,
   Uprising, unveiling, affirm
That the play is the tragedy 'Man,'
   And its hero the Conqueror Worm.

The Haunted Palace

In the greenest of our valleys
   By good angels tenanted,
Once a fair and stately palace –
   Radiant palace – reared its head.
In the monarch Thought's dominion –
   It stood there!
Never seraph spread a pinion
   Over fabric half so fair!

Banners yellow, glorious, golden,
   On its roof did float and flow,
(This – all this – was in the olden
   Time long ago);
And every gentle air that dallied,
   In that sweet day,
Along the ramparts plumed and pallid,
   A wingéd odour went away.

Wanderers in that happy valley,
   Through two luminous windows, saw
Spirits moving musically,
   To a lute's well-tunéd law,
Round about a throne where, sitting
   (Porphyrogene!)
In state his glory well-befitting,
   The ruler of the realm was seen.

And all with pearl and ruby glowing
   Was the fair palace door,
Through which came flowing, flowing, flowing,
   And sparkling evermore,
A troop of Echoes, whose sweet duty
   Was but to sing,
In voices of surpassing beauty,
   The wit and wisdom of their king.

But evil things, in robes of sorrow,
   Assailed the monarch's high estate.
(Ah, let them mourn! – for never morrow
   Shall dawn upon him desolate!)
And round about his home the glory
   That blushed and bloomed,
Is but a dim-remembered story
   Of the old time entombed.

And travellers, now, within that valley,
   Through the red-litten windows see
Vast forms, that move fantastically
   To a discordant melody,
While, like a ghastly rapid river,
   Through the pale door
A hideous throng rush out forever,
   And laugh – but smile no more.

Scenes from Politian

An Unpublished Drama

I

ROME. – *A Hall in a Palace.* ALESSANDRA and CASTIGLIONE.

ALESSANDRA. Thou art sad, Castiglione.
CASTIGLIONE. Sad! – not I.
Oh, I'm the happiest, happiest man in Rome!
A few days more, thou knowest, my Alessandra,
Will make thee mine. Oh, I am very happy!
    ALESS. Methinks thou hast a singular way of showing
Thy happiness! – what ails thee, cousin of mine?
Why didst thou sigh so deeply?
    CAS. Did I sigh?
I was not conscious of it. It is a fashion,
A silly – a most silly fashion I have
When I am *very* happy. Did I sigh?   (*Sighing.*)
    ALESS. Thou didst. Thou art not well. Thou hast indulged
Too much of late, and I am vexed to see it.
Late hours and wine, Castiglione, – these
Will ruin thee! – thou art already altered –
Thy looks are haggard – nothing so wears away
The constitution as late hours and wine.
    CAS. (*musing*). Nothing, fair cousin, nothing – not even deep
        sorrow –
Wears it away like evil hours and wine.
I will amend.
    ALESS. Do it! I would have thee drop
Thy riotous company, too – fellows low born
Ill suit the like with old Di Broglio's heir
And Alessandra's husband.
    CAS. I will drop them.
    ALESS. Thou wilt – thou must. Attend thou also more
To thy dress and equipage – they are over plain
For thy lofty rank and fashion – much depends
Upon appearances.
    CAS. I'll see to it.

ALESS. Then see to it! – pay more attention, sir,
To a becoming carriage – much thou wantest
In dignity.
    CAS. Much, much, oh, much I want
In proper dignity.
    ALESS. (*haughtily*). Thou mockest me, sir!
    CAS. (*abstractedly*). Sweet, gentle Lalage!
    ALESS. Heard I aright?
I speak to him – he speaks of Lalage!
Sir Count! (*places her hand on his shoulder*) what art thou dreaming?
       He's not well!
What ails thee, sir?
    CAS. (*starting*). Cousin! fair cousin! – madam!
I crave thy pardon – indeed I am not well –
Your hand from off my shoulder, if you please.
This air is most oppressive! – Madam – the Duke!

Enter DI BROGLIO.

DI BROGLIO. My son, I've news for thee! – hey? – what's the
       matter? (*observing* ALESSANDRA.)
I' the pouts? Kiss her, Castiglione! kiss her,
You dog! and make it up, I say, this minute!
I've news for you both. Politian is expected
Hourly in Rome – Politian, Earl of Leicester!
We'll have him at the wedding. 'Tis his first visit
To the imperial city.
    ALESS. What! Politian
Of Britain, Earl of Leicester?
    DI BROG. The same, my love.
We'll have him at the wedding. A man quite young
In years, but grey in fame. I have not seen him,
But rumor speaks of him as of a prodigy
Pre-eminent in arts, and arms, and wealth,
And high descent. We'll have him at the wedding.
    ALESS. I have heard much of this Politian.
Gay, volatile and giddy – is he not?
And little given to thinking.

25

DI BROG. Far from it, love.
No branch, they say, of all philosophy
So deep abstruse he has not mastered it.
Learned as few are learned.
    ALESS. 'Tis very strange!
I have known men have seen Politian
And sought his company. They speak of him
As of one who entered madly into life,
Drinking the cup of pleasure to the dregs.
    CAS. Ridiculous! Now *I* have seen Politian
And know him well – nor learned nor mirthful he.
He is a dreamer, and a man shut out
From common passions.
    DI BROG. Children, we disagree.
Let us go forth and taste the fragrant air
Of the garden. Did I dream, or did I hear
Politian was a *melancholy* man?   (*Exeunt.*)

II

ROME. – *A Lady's apartment, with a window open and looking into a
    garden.* LALAGE, *in deep mourning, reading at a table on which lie
    some books and a hand-mirror. In the background* JACINTA *(a
    servant maid) leans carelessly upon a chair.*

    LAL. Jacinta! is it thou?
    JAC.. (*pertly*). Yes, ma'am, I'm here.
    LAL. I did not know, Jacinta, you were in waiting.
Sit down! – let not my presence trouble you –
Sit down! – for I am humble, most humble.
    JAC. (*aside*). 'Tis time.
        (JACINTA *seats herself in a sidelong manner upon the chair, resting
    her elbows upon the back, and regarding her mistress with a con-
    temptuous look.* LALAGE *continues to read.*)
    LAL. 'It in another climate, so he said,
Bore a bright golden flower, but not i' this soil!'
        (*Pauses, turns over some leaves, and resumes.*)

26

'No lingering winters there, nor snow, nor shower –
But Ocean ever to refresh mankind
Breathes the shrill spirit of the western wind.'
Oh, beautiful! – most beautiful! – how like
To what my fevered soul doth dream of Heaven!
O happy land! (*Pauses*.) She died! – the maiden died!
O still more happy maiden who couldst die!
Jacinta!

      (JACINTA *returns no answer, and* LALAGE *presently resumes*.)
      Again! – a similar tale
Told of a beauteous dame beyond the sea!
Thus speaketh one Ferdinand in the words of the play –
'She died full young' – one Bossola answers him –
'I think not so – her infelicity
Seemed to have years too many' – Ah, luckless lady!
Jacinta!   (*Still no answer*.)
      Here's a far sterner story –
But like – oh, very like in its despair –
Of that Egyptian queen, winning so easily
A thousand hearts – losing at length her own.
She died. Thus endeth the history – and her maids
Lean over her and weep – two gentle maids
With gentle names – Eiros and Charmion!
Rainbow and Dove! – Jacinta!

    JAC. (*pettishly*). Madam, what *is* it?
    LAL. Wilt thou, my good Jacinta, be so kind
As go down in the library and bring me
The Holy Evangelists.
    JAC. Pshaw!   (*Exit*.)
    LAL. If there be balm
For the wounded spirit in Gilead it is there!
Dew in the night time of my bitter trouble
Will there be found – 'dew sweeter far than that
Which hangs like chains of pearl on Hermon hill.'

        (*Re-enter* JACINTA, *and throws a volume on the table*.)
    LAL. (*astonished*). What didst thou say, Jacinta? Have I done
      aught
To grieve thee or to vex thee? – I am sorry.

27

For thou hast served me long and ever been
Trustworthy and respectful.   (*Resumes her reading.*)
     JAC. I can't believe
She has any more jewels – no – no – she gave me all.

                                                      (*Aside.*)
     LAL. What didst thou say, Jacinta? Now I bethink me,
Thou hast not spoken lately of thy wedding.
How fares good Ugo? – and when is it to be?
Can I do aught? – is there no further aid
Thou needest, Jacinta?
     JAC. Is there no *further* aid!
That's meant for me. (*Aside.*) I'm sure, madam, you need not
Be always throwing those jewels in my teeth.
     LAL. Jewels! Jacinta – now indeed, Jacinta,
I thought not of the jewels.
     JAC. Oh! perhaps not!
But then I might have sworn it. After all,
There's Ugo says the ring is only paste,
For he's sure the Count Castiglione never
Would have given a real diamond to such as you;
And at the best I'm certain, madam, you cannot
Have use for jewels *now*. But I might have sworn it.

                                                      (*Exit.*)
                    (LALAGE *bursts into tears, and leans her head*
                         upon the table – after a short pause raises it.)
     LAL. Poor Lalage! – and is it come to this?
Thy servant maid! – but courage! – 'tis but a viper
Whom thou hast cherished to sting thee to the soul!

                                                      (*Taking up the mirror.*)
Ha! here at least's a friend – too much a friend
In earlier days – a friend will not deceive thee.
Fair mirror and true! now tell me (for thou canst)
A tale – a pretty tale – and heed thou not
Though it be rife with wo. It answers me.
It speaks of sunken eyes, and wasted cheeks,
And Beauty long deceased – remembers me
Of Joy departed – Hope, the Seraph Hope,
Inurned and entombed! – now, in a tone

Low, sad, and solemn, but most audible,
Whispers of early grave untimely yawning
For ruined maid. Fair mirror and true! – thou liest not!
Thou hast no end to gain – no heart to break –
Castiglione lied who said he loved –
Thou true – he false! – false! – false!

> (*While she speaks a monk enters her apartment and
> approaches unobserved.*)

MONK. Refuge thou hast,
Sweet daughter! in Heaven. Think of eternal things!
Give up thy soul to penitence, and pray!

LAL. (*arising hurriedly*). I *cannot* pray! – My soul is at war with
    God!
The frightful sounds of merriment below
Disturb my senses – go! I cannot pray –
The sweet airs from the garden worry me!
Thy presence grieves me – go! – thy priestly raiment
Fills me with dread – thy ebony crucifix
With horror and awe!

MONK. Think of thy precious soul!

LAL. Think of my early days! – think of my father
And mother in Heaven! think of our quiet home,
And the rivulet that ran before the door!
Think of my little sisters! – think of them!
And think of me! – think of my trusting love
And confidence – his vows – my ruin, think – think
Of my unspeakable misery! — begone!
Yet stay! yet stay! – what was it thou saidst of prayer
And penitence? Didst thou not speak of faith
And vows before the throne?

MONK. I did.

LAL. 'Tis well.
There *is* a vow were fitting should be made –
A sacred vow, imperative, and urgent,
A solemn vow!

MONK. Daughter, this zeal is well!

LAL. Father, this zeal is anything but well!
Hast thou a crucifix fit for this thing?

29

A crucifix whereon to register
This sacred vow?   (*He hands her his own.*)
Not that! – Oh! no! – no! – no!   (*Shuddering.*)
Not that! Not that! – I tell thee, holy man.
Thy raiments and thy ebony cross affright me!
Stand back! I have a crucifix myself, –
I have a crucifix! Methinks 'twere fitting
The deed – the vow – the symbol of the deed –
And the deed's register should tally, father!
          (*Draws a cross-handled dagger and raises it on high.*)
Behold the cross wherewith a vow like mine
Is written in Heaven!
   MONK. Thy words are madness, daughter,
And speak a purpose unholy – thy lips are livid –
Thine eyes are wild – tempt not the wrath divine!
Pause ere too late! – oh, be not – be not rash!
Swear not the oath – oh, swear it not!
   LAL. 'Tis sworn!

III

An apartment in a palace. POLITIAN *and* BALDAZZAR.

   BALDAZZAR. Arouse thee now, Politian!
Thou must not – nay indeed, indeed, thou shalt not
Give way unto these humors. Be thyself!
Shake off the idle fancies that beset thee,
And live, for now thou diest!
   POLITIAN. Not so, Baldazzar!
Surely I live.
   BAL. Politian, it doth grieve me
To see thee thus.
   POL. Baldazzar, it doth grieve me
To give thee cause for grief, my honored friend.
Command me, sir! what wouldst thou have me do?
At thy behest I will shake off that nature
Which from my forefathers I did inherit,
Which with my mother's milk I did imbibe,

30

And be no more Politian, but some other.
Command me, sir!
    BAL. To the field then – to the field –
To the senate or the field.
    POL. Alas! alas!
There is an imp would follow me even there!
There is an imp *hath* followed me even there!
There is — what voice was that?
    BAL. I heard it not.
I heard not any voice except thine own,
And the echo of thine own.
    POL. Then I but dreamed.
    BAL. Give not thy soul to dreams: the camp – the court
Befit thee – Fame awaits thee – Glory calls –
And her the trumpet-tongued thou wilt not hear
In hearkening to imaginary sounds
And phantom voices.
    POL. It *is* a phantom voice!
Didst thou not hear it *then?*
    BAL. I heard it not.
    POL. Thou heardst it not! — Baldazzar, speak no more
To me, Politian, of thy camps and courts.
Oh! I am sick, sick, sick, even unto death,
Of the hollow and high-sounding vanities
Of the populous Earth! Bear with me yet awhile!
We have been boys together – school-fellows –
And now are friends – yet shall not be so long –
For in the eternal city thou shalt do me
A kind and gentle office, and a Power –
A Power august, benignant, and supreme –
Shall then absolve thee of all further duties
Unto thy friend.
    BAL. Thou speakest a fearful riddle
I *will* not understand.
    POL. Yet now as Fate
Approaches, and the Hours are breathing low,
The sands of time are changed to golden grains,
And dazzle me, Baldazzar. Alas! alas!

I *cannot* die, having within my heart
So keen a relish for the beautiful
As hath been kindled within it. Methinks the air
Is balmier now than it was wont to be –
Rich melodies are floating in the winds –
A rarer loveliness bedecks the earth –
And with a holier lustre the quiet moon
Sitteth in Heaven. – Hist! hist! thou canst not say
Thou hearest not *now*, Baldazzar?
    BAL. Indeed I hear not.
    POL. Not hear it! – listen now – listen! – the faintest sound
And yet the sweetest that ear ever heard!
A lady's voice! – and sorrow in the tone!
Baldazzar, it oppresses me like a spell!
Again! – again! – how solemnly it falls
Into my heart of hearts! that eloquent voice
Surely I never heard – yet it were well
Had I *but* heard it with its thrilling tones
In earlier days!
    BAL. I myself hear it now.
Be still! – the voice, if I mistake not greatly,
Proceeds from yonder lattice – which you may see
Very plainly through the window – it belongs,
Does it not? unto this palace of the Duke.
The singer is undoubtedly beneath
The roof of his Excellency – and perhaps
Is even that Alessandra of whom he spoke
As the betrothed of Castiglione,
His son and heir.
    POL. Be still! – it comes again!
    VOICE (*very faintly*).
>   'And is thy heart so strong
>   As for to leave me thus,
>   Who have loved thee so long
>   In wealth and wo among?
>   And is thy heart so strong
>   As for to leave me thus?
>   Say nay – say nay!'

BAL. The song is English, and I oft have heard it
In merry England – never so plaintively –
Hist! hist! it comes again!

    Voice (*more loudly*). 'Is it so strong
             As for to leave me thus,
             Who have loved thee so long
             In wealth and wo among?
             And is thy heart so strong
             As for to leave me thus?
                       Say nay – say nay!'

BAL. 'Tis hushed and all is still!

POL. All *is not* still.

BAL. Let us go down.

POL. Go down, Baldazzar, go!

BAL. The hour is growing late – the Duke awaits us, –
Thy presence is expected in the hall
Below. What ails thee, Earl Politian?

    VOICE (*distinctly*). 'Who have loved thee so long,
             In wealth and wo among!
             And is thy heart so strong?
                     Say nay – say nay!'

BAL. Let us descend! – 'tis time. Politian, give
These fancies to the wind. Remember, pray,
Your bearing lately savored much of rudeness
Unto the Duke. Arouse thee! and remember!

    POL. Remember? I do. Lead on! I *do* remember.

                                  (*Going.*)

Let us descend. Believe me I would give,
Freely would give the broad lands of my earldom
To look upon the face hidden by yon lattice –
'To gaze upon that veiled face, and hear
Once more that silent tongue.'

    BAL. Let me beg you, sir,
Descend with me – the Duke may be offended.
Let us go down, I pray you.

    VOICE (*loudly*). *Say nay! say nay!*

    POL. (*aside*). 'Tis strange! – 'tis very strange – methought the
      voice

Chimed in with my desires and bade me stay!
(*Approaching the window.*)
Sweet voice! I heed thee, and will surely stay.
Now be this Fancy, by Heaven, or be it Fate,
Still will I not descend. Baldazzar, make
Apology unto the Duke for me;
I go not down to-night.
    BAL. Your lordship's pleasure
Shall be attended to. Good-night, Politian.
    POL. Good-night, my friend, good-night.

IV

The gardens of a palace – moonlight. LALAGE *and* POLITIAN.

    LALAGE. And dost thou speak of love
To *me*, Politian? – dost thou speak of love
To Lalage? – ah, wo – ah, wo is me!
This mockery is most cruel – most cruel indeed!
    POLITIAN. Weep not! oh, sob not thus! – thy bitter tears
Will madden me. Oh, mourn not, Lalage –
Be comforted! I know – I know it all,
And *still* I speak of love. Look at me, brightest
And beautiful Lalage! – turn here thine eyes!
Thou askest me if I could speak of love,
Knowing what I know, and seeing what I have seen.
Thou askest me that – and thus I answer thee –
Thus on my bended knee I answer thee.   (*Kneeling.*)
Sweet Lalage, *I love thee – love thee – love thee;*
Thro' good and ill – thro' weal and wo *I love thee.*
Not mother, with her first-born on her knee,
Thrills with intenser love than I for thee.
Not on God's altar, in any time or clime,
Burned there a holier fire than burneth now
Within my spirit for *thee.* And do I love?   (*Arising.*)
Even for thy woes I love – even for thy woes –
Thy beauty and thy woes.

LAL. Alas! proud Earl,
Thou dost forget thyself, remembering me!
How, in thy father's halls, among the maidens
Pure and reproachless of thy princely line,
Could the dishonored Lalage abide?
Thy wife, and with a tainted memory –
My seared and blighted name, how would it tally
With the ancestral honors of thy house,
And with thy glory?
    POL. Speak not to me of glory!
I hate – I loathe the name; I do abhor
The unsatisfactory and ideal thing.
Art thou not Lalage, and I Politian?
Do I not love – art thou not beautiful –
What need we more? Ha! glory! – now speak not of it:
By all I hold most sacred and most solemn –
By all my wishes now – my fears hereafter –
By all I scorn on earth and hope in heaven –
There is no deed I would more glory in,
Than in thy cause to scoff at this same glory
And trample it under foot. What matters it –
What matters it, my fairest, and my best,
That we go down unhonored and forgotten
Into the dust – so we descend together.
Descend together – and then – and then perchance –
    LAL. Why dost thou pause, Politian?
    POL. And then perchance
Arise together, Lalage, and roam
The starry and quiet dwellings of the blest,
And still –
    LAL. Why dost thou pause, Politian?
    POL. And still *together – together*.
    LAL. Now, Earl of Leicester!
Thou *lovest* me, and in my heart of hearts
I feel thou lovest me truly.
    POL. Oh, Lalage!

                    (*Throwing himself upon his knee.*)
And lovest thou *me?*

LAL. Hist! hush! within the gloom
Of yonder trees methought a figure past –
A spectral figure, solemn, and slow, and noiseless –
Like the grim shadow Conscience, solemn and noiseless.

(*Walks across and returns.*)

I was mistaken – 'twas but a giant bough
Stirred by the autumn wind. Politian!

POL. My Lalage – my love! why art thou moved?
Why dost thou turn so pale? Not Conscience' self,
Far less a shadow which thou likenest to it,
Should shake the firm spirit thus. But the night wind
Is chilly – and these melancholy boughs
Throw over all things a gloom.

LAL. Politian!
Thou speakest to me of love. Knowest thou the land
With which all tongues are busy – a land new found –
Miraculously found by one of Genoa –
A thousand leagues within the golden west?
A fairy land of flowers, and fruit, and sunshine,
And crystal lakes, and over-arching forests,
And mountains, around whose towering summits the
        winds
Of Heaven untrammelled flow – which air to breathe
Is Happiness now, and will be Freedom hereafter
In days that are to come?

POL. Oh, wilt thou – wilt thou
Fly to that Paradise – my Lalage, wilt thou
Fly thither with me? There Care shall be forgotten
And Sorrow shall be no more, and Eros be all.
And life shall then be mine, for I will live
For thee, and in thine eyes – and thou shalt be
No more a mourner – but the radiant Joys
Shall wait upon thee, and the angel Hope
Attend thee ever; and I will kneel to thee
And worship thee, and call thee my beloved,
My own, my beautiful, my love, my wife,
My all; – oh, wilt thou – wilt thou, Lalage,
Fly thither with me?

36

LAL. A deed is to be done –
Castiglione lives!
  POL. And he shall die! (*Exit.*)
  LAL. (*after a pause*). And – he – shall – die! — alas!
Castiglione die! Who spoke the words?
Where am I? – what was it he said? – Politian!
Thou *art* not gone – thou art not *gone*, Politian!
I *feel* thou art not gone – yet dare not look,
Lest I behold thee not – thou *couldst* not go
With those words upon thy lips – Oh, speak to me!
And let me hear thy voice – one word – one word,
To say thou art not gone, – one little sentence,
To say how thou dost scorn – how thou dost hate
My womanly weakness. Ha! ha! thou *art* not gone –
Oh, speak to me! I *knew* thou wouldst not go!
I knew thou wouldst not, couldst not, *durst* not go.
Villain, thou *art* not gone – thou mockest me!
And thus I clutch thee – thus! — He is gone, he is gone –
Gone – gone. Where am I? — 'tis well – 'tis very well!
So that the blade be keen – the blow be sure,
'Tis well, 'tis *very* well – alas! alas!

V

The suburbs. POLITIAN *alone.*

POLITIAN. This weakness grows upon me. I am faint,
And much I fear me ill – it will not do
To die ere I have lived! – Stay – stay thy hand,
O Azrael, yet awhile! – Prince of the Powers
Of Darkness and the Tomb, Oh, pity me!
Oh, pity me! let me not perish now,
In the budding of my Paradisal Hope!
Give me to live yet – yet a little while:
'Tis I who pray for life – I who so late
Demanded but to die – what sayeth the Count?

Enter BALDAZZAR.

BALDAZZAR. That, knowing no cause of quarrel or of feud
Between the Earl Politian and himself,
He doth decline your cartel.

POL. *What* didst thou say?
What answer was it you brought me, good Baldazzar?
With what excessive fragrance the zephyr comes
Laden from yonder bowers! – a fairer day,
Or one more worthy Italy, methinks
No mortal eyes have seen! – *What* said the Count?

BAL. That he, Castiglione, not being aware
Of any feud existing, or any cause
Of quarrel between your lordship and himself,
Cannot accept the challenge.

POL. It is most true –
All this is very true. When saw you, sir,
When saw you, now, Baldazzar, in the frigid
Ungenial Britain which we left so lately,
A heaven so calm as this – so utterly free
From the evil taint of clouds? – And he did *say?*

BAL. No more, my lord, than I have told you, sir:
The Count Castiglione will not fight,
Having no cause for quarrel.

POL. Now this is true –
All very true. Thou art my friend, Baldazzar,
And I have not forgotten it – thou'lt do me
A piece of service; wilt thou go back and say
Unto this man, that I, the Earl of Leicester,
Hold him a villain? – thus much, I prythee, say
Unto the Count – it is exceeding just
He should have cause for quarrel.

BAL. My lord! – my friend! ——

POL. (*aside*). 'Tis he – he comes himself! (*Aloud*.) Thou reasonest
      well.
I know what thou wouldst say – not send the message –
Well! I will think of it – I will not send it.
Now prythee, leave me – hither doth come a person
With whom affairs of a most private nature
I would adjust.

38

BAL. I go – to-morrow we meet,
Do we not? – at the Vatican.
    POL. At the Vatican.   (*Exit* BALDAZZAR.)

                Enter CASTIGLIONE.

    CAS. The Earl of Leicester here!
    POL. I *am* the Earl of Leicester, and thou seest,
Dost thou not, that I am here?
    CAS. My lord, some strange,
Some singular mistake – misunderstanding –
Hath without doubt arisen: thou hast been urged
Thereby, in heat of anger, to address
Some words most unaccountable, in writing,
To me, Castiglione; the bearer being
Baldazzar, Duke of Surrey. I am aware
Of nothing which might warrant thee in this thing,
Having given thee no offence. Ha! – am I right?
'Twas a mistake? – undoubtedly – we all
Do err at times.
    POL. Draw, villain, and prate no more!
    CAS. Ha! – draw? – and villain? have at thee then at once,
Proud Earl!   (*Draws.*)
    POL. (*drawing*). Thus to the expiatory tomb,
Untimely sepulchre, I do devote thee
In the name of Lalage!
    CAS. (*Letting fall his sword and recoiling to the extremity of the
        stage*). Of Lalage!
Hold off – thy sacred hand! – avaunt I say!
Avaunt – I will not fight thee – indeed I dare not.
    POL. Thou wilt not fight with me, didst say, Sir Count?
Shall I be baffled thus? – now this is well;
Didst say thou *darest* not? Ha!
    CAS. I dare not – dare not –
Hold off thy hand – with that beloved name
So fresh upon thy lips I will not fight thee –
I cannot – dare not.
    POL. Now by my halidom
I do believe thee! – coward, I do believe thee!

                            39

CAS. Ha! – coward! – this may not be!
(*Clutches his sword and staggers towards* POLITIAN, *but his purpose is changed before reaching him, and he falls upon his knee at the feet of the Earl*.)
                    Alas! my lord,
It is – it is – most true. In such a cause
I am the veriest coward. Oh, pity me!
    POL. (*greatly softened*). Alas! – I do – indeed I pity thee.
    CAS. And Lalage —
    POL. *Scoundrel!* – *arise and die!*
    CAS. It needeth not be – thus – thus – Oh, let me die
Thus on my bended knee. It were most fitting
That in this deep humiliation I perish.
For in the fight I will not raise a hand
Against thee, Earl of Leicester. Strike thou home –
                                            (*Baring his bosom.*)
Here is no let or hindrance to thy weapon –
Strike home. I *will not* fight thee.
    POL. Now s'Death and Hell!
Am I not – am I not sorely – grievously tempted
To take thee at thy word? But mark me, sir!
Think not to fly me thus. Do thou prepare
For public insult in the streets – before
The eyes of the citizens. I'll follow thee –
Like an avenging spirit I'll follow thee
Even unto death. Before those whom thou lovest –
Before all Rome I'll taunt thee, villain, – I'll taunt thee,
Dost hear? with *cowardice* – thou *wilt not* fight me?
Thou liest! thou *shalt!*   (*Exit.*)
    CAS. Now this indeed is just!
Most righteous, and most just, avenging Heaven!

POEMS WRITTEN IN YOUTH

Sonnet to Science

Science! true daughter of Old Time thou art!
   Who alterest all things with thy peering eyes.
Why preyest thou thus upon the poet's heart,
   Vulture, whose wings are dull realities?
How should he love thee? or how deem thee wise,
   Who wouldst not leave him in his wandering
To seek for treasure in the jewelled skies,
   Albeit he soared with an undaunted wing?
Hast thou not dragged Diana from her car?
   And driven the Hamadryad from the wood
To seek a shelter in some happier star?
   Hast thou not torn the Naiad from her flood,
The Elfin from the green grass, and from me
   The summer dream beneath the tamarind tree?

Al Aaraaf[1]

PART I

Oh! nothing earthly save the ray
(Thrown back from flowers) of Beauty's eye,
As in those gardens where the day
Springs from the gems of Circassy –
Oh! nothing earthly save the thrill
Of melody in woodland rill –
Or (music of the passion-hearted)

---

[1] A star was discovered by Tycho Brahe which appeared suddenly in the heavens
– attained, in a few days, a brilliancy surpassing that of Jupiter – then as suddenly
disappeared, and has never been seen since.

Joy's voice so peacefully departed
That, like the murmur in the shell,
Its echo dwelleth and will dwell –
Oh! nothing of the dross of ours –
Yet all the beauty – all the flowers
That list our Love, and deck our bowers –
Adorn yon world afar, afar –
The wandering star.

'Twas a sweet time for Nesace – for there
Her world lay lolling on the golden air,
Near four bright suns – a temporary rest –
An oasis in desert of the blest.
Away – away – 'mid seas of rays that roll
Empyrean splendor o'er th' unchained soul –
The soul that scarce (the billows are so dense)
Can struggle to its destined eminence –
To distant spheres, from time to time, she rode,
And late to ours, the favor'd one of God –
But, now, the ruler of an anchor'd realm,
She throws aside the sceptre – leaves the helm,
And, amid incense and high spiritual hymns,
Laves in quadruple light her angel limbs.

Now happiest, loveliest in yon lovely Earth,
Whence sprang the 'Idea of Beauty' into birth.
(Falling in wreaths thro' many a startled star,
Like woman's hair 'mid pearls, until, afar,
It lit on hills Achaian, and there dwelt)
She looked into Infinity – and knelt.
Rich clouds, for canopies, about her curled –
Fit emblems of the model of her world –
Seen but in beauty – not impeding sight
Of other beauty glittering thro' the light –
A wreath that twined each starry form around,
And all the opal'd air in color bound.

All hurriedly she knelt upon a bed
Of flowers; of lilies such as rear'd the head

On the fair Capo Deucato,[1] and sprang
So eagerly around about to hang
Upon the flying footsteps of – deep pride –
Of her who loved a mortal – and so died.[2]
The Sephalica, budding with young bees,
Uprear'd its purple stem around her knees:
And gemmy flower, of Trebizond misnam'd[3]
Inmate of highest stars, where erst it sham'd
All other loveliness: its honied dew
(The fabled nectar that the heathen knew)
Deliriously sweet, was dropp'd from Heaven,
And fell on gardens of the unforgiven
In Trebizond – and on a sunny flower
So like its own above, that, to this hour,
It still remaineth, torturing the bee
With madness, and unwonted reverie:
In Heaven, and all its environs, the leaf
And blossom of the fairy plant, in grief
Disconsolate linger – grief that hangs her head,
Repenting follies that full long have fled,
Heaving her white breast to the balmy air,
Like guilty beauty, chasten'd, and more fair:
Nyctanthes too, as sacred as the light
She fears to perfume, perfuming the night:
And Clytia[4] pondering between many a sun,
While pettish tears adown her petals run:
And that aspiring flower that sprang on Earth[5] –

[1] On Santa Maura – olim *Deucadia*.
[2] Sappho.
[3] This flower is much noticed by Lewenhoeck and Tournefort. The bee, feeding upon its blossom, becomes intoxicated.
[4] Clytia – The *Chrysanthemum Peruvianum*, or, to employ a better known term, the *turnsol* – which turns continually towards the sun, covers itself, like Peru, the country from which it comes, with dewy clouds which cool and refresh its flowers during the most violent heat of the day. – B. de St Pierre.
[5] There is cultivated in the king's garden at Paris a species of serpentine aloes without prickles, whose large and beautiful flower exhales a strong odor of the vanilla during the time of its expansion, which is very short. It does not blow till towards the month of July; you then perceive it gradually open its petals – expand them – fade – and die. – St Pierre.

And died, ere scarce exalted into birth,
Bursting its odorous heart in spirit to wing
Its way to Heaven, from garden of a king:
And Valisnerian lotus thither flown[1]
From struggling with the waters of the Rhone:
And thy most lovely purple perfume, Zante![2]
Isola d'oro! – Fior di Levante!
And the Nelumbo bud that floats for ever[3]
With Indian Cupid down the holy river –
Fair flowers, and fairy! to whose care is given
To bear the Goddess' song, in odors, up to Heaven:[4]

        'Spirit! that dwellest where,
            In the deep sky,
        The terrible and fair,
            In beauty vie!
        Beyond the line of blue –
            The boundary of the star
        Which turneth at the view
            Of thy barrier and thy bar –
        Of the barrier overgone
            By the comets who were cast
        From their pride, and from their throne,
            To be drudges till the last –
        To be carriers of fire
            (The red fire of their heart)
        With speed that may not tire,
            And with pain that shall not part –
        Who livest – *that* we know –
            In Eternity – we feel –
        But the shadow of whose brow

[1] There is found, in the Rhone, a beautiful lily of the Valisnerian kind. Its stem will stretch to the length of three or four feet – thus preserving its head above water in the swellings of the river.
[2] The Hyacinth.
[3] It is a fiction of the Indians that Cupid was first seen floating in one of these down the river Ganges, and that he still loves the cradle of his childhood.
[4] And golden vials full of odors, which are the prayers of the saints. – *Revelation of St John.*

44

What spirit shall reveal?
Tho' the beings whom thy Nesace,
   Thy messenger hath known
Have dream'd for thy Infinity
   A model of their own[1] –
Thy will is done, O God!
   The star hath ridden high
Thro' many a tempest, but she rode
   Beneath thy burning eye;
And here, in thought, to thee –
   In thought that can alone
Ascend thy empire and so be
   A partner of thy throne –
By winged Fantasy,[2]
   My embassy is given,
Till secrecy shall knowledge be
   In the environs of Heaven.'

She ceased – and buried then her burning cheek,
Abashed, amid the lilies there, to seek
A shelter from the fervor of His eye;
For the stars trembled at the Deity.
She stirred not – breathed not – for a voice was there
How solemnly pervading the calm air!
A sound of silence on the startled ear
Which dreamy poets name 'the music of the sphere.'
Ours is a world of words: Quiet we call
'Silence' – which is the merest word of all.
All nature speaks, and ev'n ideal things
Flap shadowy sounds from visionary wings –
But ah! not so when, thus, in realms on high
The eternal voice of God is passing by,
And the red winds are withering in the sky!

[1] The Humanitarians held that God was to be understood as having really a
human form.

   [2] Seltsamen Tochter Jovis
      Seinem Schosskinde
      Der Phantasie. – Goethe

'What tho' in worlds which sightless cycles run,[1]
Link'd to a little system, and one sun –
Where all my love is folly and the crowd
Still think my terrors but the thunder-cloud,
The storm, the earthquake, and the ocean-wrath –
(Ah! will they cross my in my angrier path?)
What tho' in worlds which own a single sun
The sands of Time grow dimmer as they run,
Yet thine is my resplendency, so given
To bear my secrets thro' the upper Heaven.
Leave tenantless thy crystal home, and fly,
With all thy train, athwart the moony sky –
Apart – like fireflies in Sicilian night,[2]
And wing to other worlds another light!
Divulge the secrets of thy embassy
To the proud orbs that twinkle – and so be
To ev'ry heart a barrier and a ban
Lest the stars totter in the guilt of man!'

Up rose the maiden in the yellow night,
The single-mooned eve! – on Earth we plight
Our faith to one love – and one moon adore –
The birthplace of young Beauty had no more.
As sprang that yellow star from downy hours,
Up rose the maiden from her shrine of flowers,
And bent o'er sheeny mountain and dim plain
Her way – but left not yet her Therasæan reign.[3]

[1] Sightless – too small to be seen. – Legge.
[2] I have often noticed a peculiar movement of the fireflies; – they will collect in a body and fly off, from a common centre, into innumerable radii.
[3] Therasæa, or Therasea, the island mentioned by Seneca, which, in a moment, arose from the sea to the eyes of astonished mariners.

PART II

High on a mountain of enamelléd head –
Such as the drowsy shepherd on his bed
Of giant pasturage lying at his ease,
Raising his heavy eyelid, starts and sees
With many a muttered 'hope to be forgiven'
What time the moon is quadrated in Heaven –
Of rosy head, that towering far away
Into the sunlit ether, caught the ray
Of sunken suns at eve – at noon of night,
While the moon danced with the fair stranger light –
Upreared upon such height arose a pile
Of gorgeous columns on th' unburthen'd air,
Flashing from Parian marble that twin smile
Far down upon the wave that sparkled there,
And nursled the young mountain in its lair.
Of molten stars their pavement, such as fall[1]
Thro' the ebon air, besilvering the pall
Of their own dissolution, while they die –
Adorning then the dwellings of the sky.
A dome, by linked light from Heaven let down,
Sat gently on these columns as a crown –
A window of one circular diamond, there,
Look'd out above into the purple air,
And rays from God shot down that meteor chain
And hallow'd all the beauty twice again,
Save when, between th' Empyrean and that ring,
Some eager spirit flapp'd his dusky wing.
But on the pillars Seraph eyes have seen
The dimness of this world: that grayish green
That nature loves the best for Beauty's grave
Lurked in each cornice, round each architrave –
And every sculptured cherub thereabout
That from his marble dwelling peeréd out,

[1] Some star which, from the ruin'd roof
Of shak'd Olympus, by mischance, did fall. – Milton

Seemed earthly in the shadow of his niche –
Achaian statues in a world so rich?
Friezes from Tadmor and Persepolis[1] –
From Baalbec, and the stilly, clear abyss
Of beautiful Gomorrha! O, the wave[2]
Is now upon thee – but too late to save!

Sound loves to revel in a summer night:
Witness the murmur of the gray twilight
That stole upon the ear, in Eyraco,[3]
Of many a wild star-gazer long ago –
That stealeth ever on the ear of him
Who, musing, gazeth on the distance dim,
And sees the darkness coming as a cloud –
Is not its form – its voice – most palpable and loud?[4]

But what is this! – it cometh – and it brings
A music with it – 'tis the rush of wings –
A pause – and then a sweeping, falling strain,
And Nesace is in her halls again.
From the wild energy of wanton haste
    Her cheeks were flushing, and her lips apart;
And zone that clung around her gentle waist
    Had burst beneath the heaving of her heart.
Within the centre of that hall to breathe

[1] Voltaire, in speaking of Persepolis, says, 'Je connois bien l'admiration qu'inspirent ces ruines – mais un palais erigé au pied d'une chaine des rochers sterils – peut il être un chef d'œuvre des arts!'
[2] 'O, the wave' – Ula Deguisi is the Turkish appellation; but, on its own shores, it is called Bahar Loth, or Almotanah. There were undoubtedly more than two cities engulphed in the 'Dead Sea.' In the Valley of Siddim were five – Admah, Zeboim, Zoar, Sodom, and Gomorrha. Stephen of Byzantium mentions eight, and Strabo thirteen (engulphed) – but the last is out of all reason.
    It is said [Tacitus, Strabo, Josephus, Daniel of St Saba, Nau, Maundrell, Troilo, D'Arvieux] that after an excessive drought, the vestiges of columns, walls, &c., are seen above the surface. At *any* season, such remains may be discovered by looking down into the transparent lake, and at such distances as would argue the existence of many settlements in the space now usurped by the 'Asphaltites.'
[3] Eyraco – Chaldea.
[4] I have often thought I could distinctly hear the sound of the darkness as it stole over the horizon.

48

She paus'd and panted, Zanthe! all beneath
The fairy light that kiss'd her golden hair,
And long'd to rest, yet could but sparkle there!

Young flowers were whispering in melody[1]
To happy flowers that night – and tree to tree:
Fountains were gushing music as they fell
In many a star-lit grove, or moon-lit dell;
Yet silence came upon material things –
Fair flowers, bright waterfalls and angel wings –
And sound alone that from the spirit sprang
Bore burthen to the charm the maiden sang:

　　''Neath blue-bell or streamer –
　　　Or tufted wild spray
　　That keeps, from the dreamer,
　　　The moonbeam away –[2]
　　Bright beings! that ponder,
　　　With half closing eyes,
　　On the stars which your wonder
　　　Hath drawn from the skies,
　　Till they glance thro' the shade, and
　　　Come down to your brow
　　Like — eyes of the maiden
　　　Who calls on you now –
　　Arise! from your dreaming
　　　In violet bowers,
　　To duty beseeming
　　　These star-litten hours –
　　And shake from your tresses
　　　Encumber'd with dew
　　The breath of those kisses
　　　That cumber them too –

[1] 'Fairies use flowers for their charactery.' – *Merry Wives of Windsor*.
[2] In Scripture is this passage – 'The sun shall not smite thee by day, nor the moon by night.' It is perhaps not generally known that the moon, in Egypt, has the effect of producing blindness to those who sleep with the face exposed to its rays, to which circumstance the passage evidently alludes.

(O! how, without you, Love!
    Could angels be blest?)
Those kisses of true love
    That lull'd ye to rest!
Up! – shake from your wing
    Each hindering thing:
The dew of the night –
    It would weigh down your flight;
And true love caresses –
    O! leave them apart!
They are light on the tresses,
    But lead on the heart.
Ligeia! Ligeia!
    My beautiful one!
Whose harshest idea
    Will to melody run,
O! is it thy will
    On the breeze to toss?
Or, capriciously still,
    Like the lone Albatross,[1]
Incumbent on night
    (As she on the air)
To keep watch with delight
    On the harmony there?

Ligeia! wherever
    Thy image may be,
No magic shall sever
    Thy music from thee.
Thou hast bound many eyes
    In a dreamy sleep –
But the strains still arise
    Which *thy* vigilance keep –
The sound of the rain,
    Which leaps down to the flower
And dances again

[1] The Albatross is said to sleep on the wing.

In the rhythm of the shower –
The murmur that springs[1]
From the growing of grass –
Are the music of things –
But are modell'd, alas! –
Away, then, my dearest,
O! hie thee away
To springs that lie clearest
Beneath the moon-ray –
To lone lake that smiles,
In its dream of deep rest,
At the many star-isles
That enjewel its breast –
Where wild flowers, creeping,
Have mingled their shade,
On its margin is sleeping
Full many a maid –
Some have left the cool glade, and
Have slept with the bee –[2]
Arouse them, my maiden,
On moorland and lea –
Go! breathe on their slumber,
All softly in ear,
The musical number
They slumber'd to hear –
For what can awaken
An angel so soon
Whose sleep hath been taken

[1] I met with this idea in an old English tale, which I am now unable to obtain, and quote from memory: – 'The verie essence, and, as it were, springeheade and origine of all musicke is the verie pleasaunte sounde which the trees of the forest do make when they growe.'
[2] The wild bee will not sleep in the shade if there be moonlight.
  The rhyme in this verse, as in one about sixty lines before, has an appearance of affectation. It is, however, imitated from Sir W. Scott, or rather from Claud Halcro – in whose mouth I admired its effect: –
          'O! were there an island,
            Tho' ever so wild,
          Where woman might smile, and
            No man be beguiled,' &c.

Beneath the cold moon,
As the spell which no slumber
Of witchery may test,
The rhythmical number
Which lulled him to rest?'

Spirits in wing, and angels to the view,
A thousand seraphs burst th' Empyrean thro',
Young dreams still hovering on their drowsy flight –
Seraphs in all but 'Knowledge,' the keen light
That fell, refracted, thro' thy bounds, afar,
O Death! from eye of God upon that star:
Sweet was that error – sweeter still that death –
Sweet was that error – ev'n with *us* the breath
Of Science dims the mirror of our joy –
To them 'twere the Simoom, and would destroy –
For what (to them) availeth it to know
That Truth is Falsehood – or that Bliss is Woe?
Sweet was their death – with them to die was rife
With the last ecstasy of satiate life –
Beyond that death no immortality –
But sleep that pondereth and is not 'to be' –
And there – oh! may my weary spirit dwell –
Apart from Heaven's Eternity – and yet how far from Hell![1]
What guilty spirit, in what shrubbery dim,

[1] With the Arabians there is a medium between Heaven and Hell, where men suffer no punishment, but yet do not attain that tranquil and even happiness which they suppose to be characteristic of heavenly enjoyment.

> 'Un no rompido sueno –
> Un dia puro – allegre – libre
> Quiera –
> Libre de amor – de zelo –
> De odio – de esperanza – de rezelo.'
> – Luis Ponce de Leon.

Sorrow is not excluded from 'Al Aaraaf,' but it is that sorrow which the living love to cherish for the dead, and which in some minds resembles the delirium of opium. The passionate excitement of Love, and the buoyancy of spirit attendant upon intoxication, are its less holy pleasures – the price of which, to those souls who make choice of 'Al Aaraaf' as their residence after life, is final death and annihilation.

Heard not the stirring summons of that hymn?
But two: they fell: for Heaven no grace imparts
To those who hear not for their beating hearts.
A maiden angel and her seraph-lover –
O! where (and ye may seek the wide skies over)
Was Love, the blind, near sober Duty known?
Unguided Love hath fallen – 'mid 'tears of perfect moan.'[1]

He was a goodly spirit – he who fell:
A wanderer by moss-y-mantled well –
A gazer on the lights that shine above –
A dreamer in the moonbeam by his love:
What wonder? for each star is eye-like there,
And looks so sweetly down on Beauty's hair –
And they, and ev'ry mossy spring were holy
To his love-haunted heart and melancholy.
The night had found (to him a night of wo)
Upon a mountain crag, young Angelo –
Beetling it bends athwart the solemn sky,
And scowls on starry worlds that down beneath it lie.
Here sate he with his love – his dark eye bent
With eagle gaze along the firmament:
Now turned it upon her – but ever then
It trembled to the orb of Earth again.

'Ianthe, dearest, see! how dim that ray!
How lovely 'tis to look so far away!
She seem'd not thus upon that autumn eve
I left her gorgeous halls – nor mourn'd to leave.
That eve – that eve – I should remember well –
The sun-ray dropp'd, in Lemnos, with a spell
On th' Arabesque carving of a gilded hall
Wherein I sate, and on the draperied wall –
And on my eye-lids – O, the heavy light!
How drowsily it weighed them into night!

[1] 'There be tears of perfect moan
Wept for thee in Helicon.' – Milton.

53

On flowers, before, and mist, and love they ran
With Persian Saadi in his Gulistan:
But O, that light! – I slumbered – Death, the while,
Stole o'er my senses in that lovely isle
So softly that no single silken hair
Awoke that slept – or knew that he was there.

'The last spot of Earth's orb I trod upon
Was a proud temple called the Parthenon;[1]
More beauty clung around her columned wall
Than even thy glowing bosom beats withal,[2]
And when old Time my wing did disenthral
Thence sprang I – as the eagle from his tower,
And years I left behind me in an hour.
What time upon her airy bounds I hung
One half the garden of her globe was flung
Unrolling as a chart unto my view –
Tenantless cities of the desert too!
Ianthe, beauty crowded on me then,
And half I wished to be again of men.'

'My Angelo! and why of them to be?
A brighter dwelling-place is here for thee –
And greener fields than in yon world above,
And woman's loveliness – and passionate love.'

'But list, Ianthe! when the air so soft
Failed, as my pennon'd spirit leapt aloft,[3]
Perhaps my brain grew dizzy – but the world
I left so late was into chaos hurl'd,
Sprang from her station, on the winds apart,
And rolled a flame, the fiery Heaven athwart.
Methought, my sweet one, then I ceased to soar,

[1] It was entire in 1687 – the most elevated spot in Athens.
[2] 'Shadowing more beauty in their airy brows
   Than have the white breasts of the queen of love.' – Marlowe.
[3] Pennon, for pinion – Milton.

54

And fell – not swiftly as I rose before,
But with a downward, tremulous motion thro'
Light, brazen rays, this golden star unto!
Nor long the measure of my falling hours,
For nearest of all stars was thine to ours –
Dread star! that came, amid a night of mirth,
A red Dædalion on the timid Earth.'

'We came – and to thy Earth – but not to us
Be given our lady's bidding to discuss:
We came, my love; around, above, below,
Gay fire-fly of the night we come and go,
Nor ask a reason save the angel-nod
She grants to us as granted by her God –
But, Angelo, than thine grey Time unfurled
Never his fairy wing o'er fairier world!
Dim was its little disk, and angel eyes
Alone could see the phantom in the skies,
When first Al Aaraaf knew her course to be
Headlong thitherward o'er the starry sea –
But when its glory swelled upon the sky,
As glowing Beauty's bust beneath man's eye,
We paused before the heritage of men,
And thy star trembled – as doth Beauty then!'

Thus in discourse, the lovers whiled away
The night that waned and waned and brought no day.
They fell: for Heaven to them no hope imparts
Who hear not for the beating of their hearts.

Tamerlane

Kind solace in a dying hour!
   Such, father, is not (now) my theme –
I will not madly deem that power
     Of Earth may shrive me of the sin
     Unearthly pride hath revell'd in –
I have no time to dote or dream:
You call it hope – that fire of fire!
It is but agony of desire:
If I *can* hope – O God! I can –
   Its fount is holier – more divine –
I would not call thee fool, old man,
   But such is not a gift of thine.

Know thou the secret of a spirit
   Bowed from its wild pride into shame.
O yearning heart! I did inherit
   Thy withering portion with the fame,
The searing glory which hath shone
Amid the Jewels of my throne,
Halo of Hell! and with a pain
Not Hell shall make me fear again –
O craving heart, for the lost flowers
And sunshine of my summer hours!
The undying voice of that dead time,
With its interminable chime,
Rings, in the spirit of a spell,
Upon thy emptiness – a knell.

I have not always been as now:
The fevered diadem on my brow
   I claimed and won usurpingly –
Hath not the same fierce heirdom given
     Rome to the Cæsar – this to me?
     The heritage of a kingly mind,
And a proud spirit which hath striven
     Triumphantly with human kind.

On mountain soil I first drew life:
    The mists of the Taglay have shed
    Nightly their dews upon my head,
And, I believe, the winged strife
And tumult of the headlong air
Have nestled in my very hair.

So late from Heaven – that dew – it fell
    ('Mid dreams of an unholy night)
Upon me with the touch of Hell,
    While the red flashing of the light
From clouds that hung, like banners, o'er,
    Appeared to my half-closing eye
    The pageantry of monarchy;
And the deep trumpet-thunder's roar
    Came hurriedly upon me, telling
        Of human battle, where my voice,
    My own voice, silly child! – was swelling
        (O! how my spirit would rejoice,
And leap within me at the cry)
The battle-cry of Victory!

The rain came down upon my head
    Unshelter'd – and the heavy wind
    Rendered me mad and deaf and blind.
It was but man, I thought, who shed
    Laurels upon me: and the rush –
The torrent of the chilly air
Gurgled within my ear the crush
    Of empires – with the captive's prayer –
The hum of suitors – and the tone
Of flattery 'round a sovereign's throne.

My passions, from that hapless hour,
    Usurped a tyranny which men
Have deemed since I have reached to power
        My innate nature – be it so:
    But, father, there lived one who, then,
Then – in my boyhood – when their fire

Burn'd with a still intenser glow
(For passion must, with youth, expire)
    E'en *then* who knew this iron heart
    In woman's weakness had a part.

I have no words – alas! – to tell
The loveliness of loving well!
Nor would I now attempt to trace
The more than beauty of a face
Whose lineaments, upon my mind,
Are — shadows on th' unstable wind:
Thus I remember having dwelt
    Some page of early lore upon,
With loitering eye, till I have felt
The letters – with their meaning – melt
    To fantasies – with none.

O, she was worthy of all love!
    Love – as in infancy – was mine –
'Twas such as angel minds above
    Might envy: her young heart the shrine
On which my every hope and thought
    Were incense – then a goodly gift,
        For they were childish and upright –
Pure – as her young example taught:
    Why did I leave it, and, adrift,
        Trust to the fire within, for light?

We grew in age – and love – together –
    Roaming the forest, and the wild;
My breast her shield in wintry weather –
    And, when the friendly sunshine smiled.
And she would mark the opening skies,
I saw no heaven – but in her eyes.
Young Love's first lesson is — the heart;
    For 'mid that sunshine and those smiles,
When, from our little cares apart,
    And laughing at her girlish wiles,

58

I'd throw me on her throbbing breast,
  And pour my spirit out in tears –
There was no need to speak the rest –
  No need to quiet any fears
Of her – who ask'd no reason why,
But turn'd on me her quiet eye!

Yet *more* than worthy of the love
My spirit struggled with, and strove,
When, on the mountain peak, alone,
Ambition lent it a new tone –
I had no being – but in thee:
  The world and all it did contain
In the earth – the air – the sea –
  Its joy – its little lot of pain
That was new pleasure – the ideal,
  Dim, vanities of dreams by night –
And dimmer nothings which were real –
  (Shadows – and a more shadowy light!)
Parted upon their misty wings,
    And so, confusedly, became
    Thine image and – a name – a name!
Two separate – yet most intimate things.

I was ambitious – have you known
    The passion, father? You have not:
A cottager, I mark'd a throne
Of half the world as all my own,
    And murmur'd at such lowly lot –
But, just like any other dream,
    Upon the vapor of the dew
My own had past, did not the beam
    Of beauty which did while it thro'
The minute – the hour – the day – oppress
My mind with double loveliness.
We walk'd together on the crown
Of a high mountain which looked down
Afar from its proud natural towers

59

Of rock and forest, on the hills –
The dwindled hills! begirt with bowers
    And shouting with a thousand rills.

I spoke to her of power and pride,
    But mystically – in such guise
That she might deem it nought beside
    The moment's converse; in her eyes
I read, perhaps too carelessly –
    A mingled feeling with my own –
The flush on her bright cheek, to me
    Seem'd to become a queenly throne
Too well that I should let it be
    Light in the wilderness alone.

I wrapp'd myself in grandeur then,
    And donn'd a visionary crown –
        Yet it was not that Fantasy
        Had thrown her mantle over me –
But that, among the rabble – men,
    Lion Ambition is chain'd down –
And crouches to a keeper's hand –
Not so in deserts where the grand –
The wild – the terrible conspire
With their own breath to fan his fire.

Look 'round thee now on Samarcand! –
    Is she not queen of Earth? her pride
Above all cities? in her hand
    Their destinies? in all beside
Of glory which the world hath known
Stands she not nobly and alone?
Falling – her veriest stepping-stone
Shall form the pedestal of a throne –
And who her sovereign? Timour – he
    Whom the astonished people saw
Striding o'er empires haughtily
    A diadem'd outlaw!

O, human love! thou spirit given,
On Earth, of all we hope in Heaven!
Which fall'st into the soul like rain
Upon the Siroc-withered plain,
And, failing in thy power to bless,
But leav'st the heart a wilderness!
Idea! which bindest life around
With music of so strange a sound
And beauty of so wild a birth –
Farewell! for I have won the Earth.

When Hope, that eagle that tower'd, could see
    No cliff beyond him in the sky,
His pinions were bent droopingly –
    And homeward turn'd his softened eye.
'Twas sunset: when the sun will part
There comes a sullenness of heart
To him who still would look upon
The glory of the summer sun.
That soul will hate the ev'ning mist
So often lovely, and will list
To the sound of the coming darkness (known
To those whose spirits hearken) as one
Who, in a dream of night, *would* fly,
But *cannot*, from a danger nigh.

What tho' the moon – the white moon
Shed all the splendor of her noon,
Her smile is chilly – and *her* beam,
In that time of dreariness, will seem
(So like you gather in your breath)
A portrait taken after death.
And boyhood is a summer sun
Whose waning is the dreariest one –
For all we live to know is known
And all we seek to keep hath flown –
Let life, then, as the day-flower, fall
With the noon-day beauty – which is all.

I reach'd my home – my home no more –
  For all had flown who made it so.
I passed from out its mossy door,
  And, tho' my tread was soft and low,
A voice came from the threshold stone
Of one whom I had earlier known –
  O, I defy thee, Hell, to show
  On beds of fire that burn below,
  An humbler heart – a deeper wo.

Father, I firmly do believe –
  I *know* – for Death who comes for me
    From regions of the blest afar,
Where there is nothing to deceive,
    Hath left his iron gate ajar,
  And rays of truth you cannot see
  Are flashing thro' Eternity —
I do believe that Eblis hath
A snare in every human path –
Else how, when in the holy grove
I wandered of the idol, Love, –
Who daily scents his snowy wings
With incense of burnt-offerings
From the most unpolluted things
Whose pleasant bowers are yet so riven
Above with trellis'd rays from Heaven
No mote may shun – no tiniest fly –
The light'ning of his eagle eye –
How was it that Ambition crept,
  Unseen, amid the revels there,
Till growing bold, he laughed and leapt
  In the tangles of Love's very hair?

A Dream

In visions of the dark night
  I have dreamed of joy departed –
But a waking dream of life and light
  Hath left me broken-hearted.

Ah! what is not a dream by day
  To him whose eyes are cast
On things around him with a ray
  Turned back upon the past?

That holy dream – that holy dream,
  While all the world were chiding,
Hath cheered me as a lovely beam,
  A lonely spirit guiding.

What through that light, thro' storm and night,
  So trembled from afar –
What could there be more purely bright
  In Truth's day-star?

Romance

Romance, who loves to nod and sing,
With drowsy head and folded wing,
Among the green leaves as they shake
Far down within some shadowy lake,
To me a painted paroquet
Hath been – a most familiar bird –
Taught me my alphabet to say –
To lisp my very earliest word
While in the wild wood I did lie,
A child – with a most knowing eye.
Of late, eternal Condor years

So shake the very Heaven on high
With tumult as they thunder by,
I have no time for idle cares
Through gazing on the unquiet sky.
And when an hour with calmer wings
Its down upon my spirit flings –
That little time with lyre and rhyme
To while away – forbidden things!
My heart would feel to be a crime
Unless it trembled with the strings.

Fairyland

Dim vales – and shadowy floods –
And cloudy-looking woods,
Whose forms we can't discover
For the tears that drip all over
Huge moons there wax and wane –
Again – again – again –
Every moment of the night –
For ever changing places –
And they put out the star-light
With the breath from their pale faces.
About twelve by the moon-dial
One more filmy than the rest
(A kind which, upon trial,
They have found to be the best)
Comes down – still down – and down
With its centre on the crown
Of a mountain's eminence,
While its wide circumference
In easy drapery falls
Over hamlets, over halls,
Wherever they may be –
O'er the strange woods – o'er the sea –

Over spirits on the wing –
Over every drowsy thing –
And buries them up quite
In a labyrinth of light –
And then how deep! – O, deep!
Is the passion of their sleep.
In the morning they arise,
And their moony covering
Is soaring in the skies,
With the tempests as they toss,
Like — almost any thing –
Or a yellow Albatross.
They use that moon no more
For the same end as before –
Videlicet a tent –
Which I think extravagant.
Its atomies, however,
Into a shower dissever,
Of which those butterflies,
Of Earth, who seek the skies,
And so come down again
(Never-contented things!)
Have brought a specimen
Upon their quivering wings.

To ——

The bowers whereat, in dreams, I see
    The wantonest singing birds,
Are lips – and all thy melody
    Of lip-begotten words –

Thine eyes, in Heaven of heart enshrined
    Then desolately fall,
O God! on my funereal mind
    Like starlight on a pall –

Thy heart – *thy* heart! I wake and sigh,
   And sleep to dream till day
Of the truth that gold can never buy –
   Of the baubles that it may.

To the River ——

Fair river! in thy bright, clear flow
   Of crystal, wandering water,
Thou art an emblem of the glow
      Of beauty – the unhidden heart –
      The playful maziness of art
In old Alberto's daughter;

But when within thy wave she looks –
   Which glistens then, and trembles –
Why, then, the prettiest of brooks
   Her worshipper resembles;
For in his heart, as in thy stream,
   Her image deeply lies –
His heart which trembles at the beam
   Of her soul-searching eyes.

The Lake. To ——

In spring of youth it was my lot
To haunt of the wide world a spot
The which I could not love the less –
So lovely was the loneliness
Of a wild lake, with black rock bound,
And the tall pines that towered around.

But when the Night had thrown her pall
Upon that spot, as upon all,
And the mystic wind went by
Murmuring in melody –
Then – ah, then, I would awake
To the terror of the lone lake.
Yet that terror was not fright,
But a tremulous delight –
A feeling not the jewelled mine
Could teach or bribe me to define
Nor Love – although the Love were thine.

Death was in that poisonous wave,
And in its gulf a fitting grave
For him who thence could solace bring
To his lone imagining –
Whose solitary soul could make
An Eden of that dim lake.

Song

I saw thee on thy bridal day –
    When a burning blush came o'er thee,
Though happiness around thee lay,
    The world all love before thee:

And in thine eye a kindling light
    (Whatever it might be)
Was all on Earth my aching sight
    Of Loveliness could see.

That blush, perhaps, was maiden shame –
    As such it well may pass –
Though its glow hath raised a fiercer flame
    In the breast of him, alas!

Who saw thee on that bridal day,
    When that deep blush *would* come o'er thee,
Though happiness around thee lay,
    The world all love before thee.

LATER POEMS

A Dream within a Dream

Take this kiss upon the brow!
And, in parting from you now,
Thus much let me avow –
You are not wrong, who deem
That my days have been a dream;
Yet if hope has flown away
In a night, or in a day,
In a vision, or in none,
Is it therefore the less *gone?*
All that we see or seem
Is but a dream within a dream.

I stand amid the roar
Of a surf-tormented shore,
And I hold within my hand
Grains of the golden sand –
How few! yet how they creep
Through my fingers to the deep,
While I weep – while I weep!
O God! can I not grasp
Them with a tighter clasp?
O God! can I not save
One from the pitiless wave?
Is *all* that we see or seem
But a dream within a dream?

The Bells

I

Hear the sledges with the bells –
Silver bells!
What a world of merriment their melody foretells!
How they tinkle, tinkle, tinkle,
In the icy air of night!
While the stars, that oversprinkle
All the heavens, seem to twinkle
With a crystalline delight;
Keeping time, time, time,
In a sort of Runic rhyme,
To the tintinabulation that so musically wells
From the bells, bells, bells, bells,
Bells, bells, bells –
From the jingling and the tinkling of the bells.

II

Hear the mellow wedding bells,
Golden bells!
What a world of happiness their harmony foretells!
Through the balmy air of night
How they ring out their delight!
From the molten-golden notes,
And all in tune,
What a liquid ditty floats
To the turtledove that listens, while she gloats
On the moon!
Oh, from out the sounding cells,
What a gush of euphony voluminously wells!
How it swells!
How it dwells
On the Future! how it tells
Of the rapture that impels
To the swinging and the ringing

70

Of the bells, bells, bells,
Of the bells, bells, bells, bells,
Bells, bells, bells –
To the rhyming and the chiming of the bells!

III

Hear the loud alarum bells –
Brazen bells!
What a tale of terror, now, their turbulency tells!
In the startled ear of night
How they scream out their affright!
Too much horrified to speak,
They can only shriek, shriek,
Out of tune,
In a clamorous appealing to the mercy of the fire,
In a mad expostulation with the deaf and frantic fire,
Leaping higher, higher, higher,
With a desperate desire,
And a resolute endeavor
Now – now to sit or never,
By the side of the pale-faced moon.
Oh, the bells, bells, bells!
What a tale their terror tells
Of Despair!
How they clang, and clash, and roar!
What a horror they outpour
On the bosom of the palpitating air!
Yet the ear it fully knows,
By the twanging,
And the clanging,
How the danger ebbs and flows;
Yet the ear distinctly tells,
In the jangling,
And the wrangling,
How the danger sinks and swells,
By the sinking or the swelling in the anger of the bells –

Of the bells –
Of the bells, bells, bells, bells,
Bells, bells, bells –
In the clamor and the clangor of the bells!

IV

Hear the tolling of the bells –
Iron bells!
What a world of solemn thought their monody compels!
In the silence of the night,
How we shiver with affright
At the melancholy menace of their tone!
For every sound that floats
From the rust within their throats
Is a groan.
And the people – ah, the people –
They that dwell up in the steeple,
All alone,
And who tolling, tolling, tolling,
In that muffled monotone,
Feel a glory in so rolling
On the human heart a stone –
They are neither man nor woman –
They are neither brute nor human –
They are Ghouls:
And their king it is who tolls;
And he rolls, rolls, rolls,
Rolls
A pæan from the bells!
And his merry bosom swells
With the pæan of the bells!
And he dances and he yells;
Keeping time, time, time,
In a sort of Runic rhyme,
To the pæan of the bells –
Of the bells:
Keeping time, time, time,

In a sort of Runic rhyme,
    To the throbbing of the bells,
Of the bells, bells, bells –
    To the sobbing of the bells;
Keeping time, time, time,
    As he knells, knells, knells,
In a happy Runic rhyme,
    To the rolling of the bells –
Of the bells, bells, bells –
    To the tolling of the bells,
Of the bells, bells, bells, bells,
        Bells, bells, bells –
To the moaning and the groaning of the bells.

To Helen

I saw thee once – once only – years ago:
I must not say *how* many – but *not* many.
It was a July midnight; and from out
A full-orbed moon, that, like thine own soul, soaring,
Sought a precipitate pathway up through heaven,
There fell a silvery-silken veil of light,
With quietude, and sultriness, and slumber,
Upon the upturn'd faces of a thousand
Roses that grew in an enchanted garden,
Where no wind dared to stir, unless on tiptoe –
Fell on the upturn'd faces of these roses
That gave out, in return for the love-light,
Their odorous souls in an ecstatic death –
Fell on the upturned faces of these roses
That smiled and died in this parterre, enchanted
By thee, and by the poetry of thy presence.
Clad all in white, upon a violet bank
I saw thee half-reclining; while the moon
Fell on the upturn'd faces of the roses,
And on thine own, upturn'd – alas! in sorrow!

Was it not Fate, that, on this July midnight –
Was it not Fate (whose name is also Sorrow),
That bade me pause before that garden gate,
To breathe the incense of those slumbering roses?
No footstep stirred: the hated world all slept,
Save only thee and me – (O Heaven! O God!
How my heart beats in coupling those two words!)
Save only thee and me. I paused – I looked –
And in an instant all things disappeared.
(Ah, bear in mind this garden was enchanted!)
The pearly lustre of the moon went out:
The mossy banks and the meandering paths,
The happy flowers and the repining trees,
Were seen no more: the very roses' odors
Died in the arms of the adoring airs.
All – all expired save thee – save less than thou:
Save only the divine light in thine eyes –
Save but the soul in thine uplifted eyes.
I saw but them – they were the world to me.
I saw but them – saw only them for hours –
Saw only them until the moon went down.
What wild heart-histories seemed to lie enwritten
Upon those crystalline, celestial spheres!
How dark a wo! yet how sublime a hope!
How silently serene a sea of pride!
How daring an ambition! yet how deep –
How fathomless a capacity for love!

But now, at length, dear Dian sank from sight,
Into a western couch of thunder-cloud;
And thou, a ghost, amid the entombing trees
Didst glide away. *Only thine eyes remained.*
They *would not* go – they never yet have gone.
Lighting my lonely pathway home that night,
They have not left me (as my hopes have) since.
They follow me – they lead me through the years.
They are my ministers – yet I their slave.
Their office is to illumine and enkindle –

My duty, *to be saved* by their bright light,
And purified in their electric fire,
And sanctified in their elysian fire.
They fill my soul with Beauty (which is Hope),
And are far up in Heaven – the stars I kneel to
In the sad, silent watches of my night;
While even in the meridian glare of day
I see them still – two sweetly scintillant
Venuses, unextinguished by the sun!

A Valentine

For her[1] this rhyme is penned, whose luminous eyes,
    Brightly expressive as the twins of Leda,
Shall find her own sweet name, that, nestling lies
    Upon the page, enwrapped from every reader.
Search narrowly the lines! – they hold a treasure
    Divine – a talisman – an amulet
That must be worn *at heart*. Search well the measure –
    The words – the syllables! Do not forget
The trivialest point, or you may lose your labor!
    And yet there is in this no Gordian knot
Which one might not undo without a sabre,
    If one could merely comprehend the plot.
Enwritten upon the leaf where now are peering
    Eyes scintillating soul, there lie *perdus*
Three eloquent words oft uttered in the hearing
    Of poets by poets – as the name is a poet's too.
Its letters, although naturally lying
    Like the knight Pinto – Mendez Ferdinando –
Still form a synonym for Truth – Cease trying!
    You will not read the riddle, though you do the best you *can* do.

---

[1] To discover the names in this and the following poem, read the first letter of the first line in connection with the second letter of the second line, the third letter of the third line, the fourth of the fourth, and so on to the end.

An Enigma

'Seldom we find,' says Solomon Don Dunce,
  'Half an idea in the profoundest sonnet.
Through all the flimsy things we see at once
  As easily as through a Naples bonnet –
  Trash of all trash! – how *can* a lady don it?
Yet heavier far than your Petrarchan stuff –
Owl-downy nonsense that the faintest puff
  Twirls into trunk-paper the while you con it.'
And, veritably, Sol is right enough.
The general tuckermanities are arrant
Bubbles – ephemeral and *so* transparent –
  But *this* is, now – you may depend upon it –
Stable, opaque, immortal – all by dint
Of the dear names that lie concealed within't.

To —— ——

Not long ago, the writer of these lines,
In the mad pride of intellectuality,
Maintained 'the power of words' – denied that ever
A thought arose within the human brain
Beyond the utterance of the human tongue:
And now, as if in mockery of that boast,
Two words – two foreign soft dissyllables –
Italian tones, made only to be murmured
By angels dreaming in the moonlit 'dew
That hangs like chains of pearl on Hermon hill,' –
Have stirred from out the abysses of his heart,
Unthought-like thoughts that are the souls of thought,
Richer, far wilder, far diviner visions
Than even the seraph harper, Israfel,
(Who has 'the sweetest voice of all God's creatures'),
Could hope to utter. And I! my spells are broken.

The pen falls powerless from my shivering hand.
With thy dear name as text, though bidden by thee,
I cannot write – I cannot speak or think –
Alas, I cannot feel; for 'tis not feeling.
This standing motionless upon the golden
Threshold of the wide-open gate of dreams,
Gazing, entranced, adown the gorgeous vista,
And thrilling as I see, upon the right,
Upon the left, and all the way along,
Amid empurpled vapors, far away
To where the prospect terminates – *thee only*.

To my Mother

Because I feel that, in the Heavens above,
　　The angels, whispering to one another,
Can find, among their burning terms of love,
　　None so devotional as that of 'Mother,'
Therefore by that dear name I long have called you –
　　You who are more than mother unto me,
And fill my heart of hearts, where Death installed you,
　　In setting my Virginia's spirit free.
My mother – my own mother, who died early,
　　Was but the mother of myself; but you
Are mother to the one I loved so dearly,
　　And thus are dearer than the mother I knew
By that infinity with which my wife
　　Was dearer to my soul than its soul-life.

Eldorado

Gaily bedight,
A gallant knight,
In sunshine and in shadow,
Had journeyed long,
Singing a song,
In search of Eldorado.

But he grew old –
This knight so bold –
And o'er his heart a shadow
Fell as he found
No spot of ground
That looked like Eldorado.

And as his strength
Failed him at length,
He met a pilgrim shadow –
'Shadow,' said he,
'Where can it be –
This land of Eldorado?'

'Over the Mountains
Of the Moon,
Down the Valley of the Shadow,
Ride, boldly ride,'
The shade replied, –
'If you seek for Eldorado!'

To ——

I heed not that my earthly lot
    Hath – little of Earth in it –
That years of love have been forgot
    In the hatred of a minute: –
I mourn not that the desolate
    Are happier, sweet, than I,
But that *you* sorrow for *my* fate
    Who am a passer-by.

To M. L. S——

Of all who hail thy presence as the morning –
Of all to whom thine absence is the night –
The blotting utterly from out high heaven
The sacred sun – of all who, weeping, bless thee
Hourly for hope – for life – ah! above all,
For the resurrection of deep-buried faith
In Truth – in Virtue – in Humanity –
Of all who, on Despair's unhallowed bed
Lying down to die, have suddenly arisen
At thy soft-murmured words, 'Let there be light!'
At the soft-murmured words that were fulfilled
In the seraphic glancing of thine eyes –
Of all who owe thee most – whose gratitude
Nearest resembles worship – oh, remember
The truest – the most fervently devoted,
And think that these weak lines are written by him –
By him who, as he pens them, thrills to think
His spirit is communing with an angel's.

For Annie

Thank Heaven! the crisis –
   The danger is past,
And the lingering illness
   Is over at last –
And the fever called 'Living'
   Is conquered at last.

Sadly, I know
   I am shorn of my strength,
And no muscle I move
   As I lie at full length –
But no matter! – I feel
   I am better at length.

And I rest so composedly,
   Now, in my bed,
That any beholder
   Might fancy me dead –
Might start at beholding me,
   Thinking me dead.

The moaning and groaning,
   The sighing and sobbing,
Are quieted now,
   With that horrible throbbing
At heart; – ah, that horrible,
   Horrible throbbing!

The sickness – the nausea –
   The pitiless pain –
Have ceased, with the fever
   That maddened my brain –
With the fever called 'Living'
   That burned in my brain.

And oh! of all tortures
    That torture the worst
Has abated – the terrible
    Torture of thirst,
For the naphthaline river
    Of Passion accurst: –
I have drank of a water
    That quenches all thirst: –

Of a water that flows,
    With a lullaby sound,
From a spring but a very few
    Feet under ground –
From a cavern not very far
    Down under ground.

And ah! let it never
    Be foolishly said
That my room it is gloomy
    And narrow my bed;
For man never slept
    In a different bed –
And, to *sleep*, you must slumber
    In just such a bed.

My tantalised spirit
    Here blandly reposes,
Forgetting, or never
    Regretting its roses –
Its old agitations
    Of myrtles and roses:

For now, while so quietly
    Lying, it fancies
A holier odor
    About it, of pansies –
A rosemary odor,
    Commingled with pansies –

With rue and the beautiful
    Puritan pansies.

And so it lies happily,
    Bathing in many
A dream of the truth
    And the beauty of Annie –
Drowned in a bath
    Of the tresses of Annie.

She tenderly kissed me,
    She fondly caressed,
And then I fell gently
    To sleep on her breast –
Deeply so sleep
    From the heaven of her breast.

When the light was extinguished,
    She covered me warm,
And she prayed to the angels
    To keep me from harm –
To the queen of the angels
    To shield me from harm.

And I lie so composedly,
    Now, in my bed,
(Knowing her love)
    That you fancy me dead –
And I rest so contentedly,
    Now in my bed,
(With her love at my breast)
    That you fancy me dead –
That you shudder to look at me,
    Thinking me dead: –

But my heart it is brighter
    Than all of the many
Stars in the sky,

For it sparkles with Annie –
It glows with the light –
Of the love of my Annie –
With the thought of the light
Of the eyes of my Annie.

Ulalume

The skies they were ashen and sober;
The leaves they were crispèd and sere –
The leaves they were withering and sere;
It was night in the lonesome October
Of my most immemorial year;
It was hard by the dim lake of Auber,
In the misty mid region of Weir –
It was down by the dank tarn of Auber,
In the ghoul-haunted woodland of Weir.

Here once, through an alley Titanic,
Of cypress, I roamed with my Soul –
Of cypress, with Psyche, my Soul.
These were days when my heart was volcanic
As the scoriac rivers that roll –
As the lavas that restlessly roll
Their sulphurous currents down Yaanek
In the ultimate climes of the pole –
That groan as they roll down Mount Yaanek
In the realms of the boreal pole.

Our talk had been serious and sober,
But our thoughts they were palsied and sere –
Our memories were treacherous and sere –
For we knew not the month was October,
And we marked not the night of the year –
(Ah, night of all nights in the year!)

We noted not the dim lake of Auber –
　　(Though once we had journeyed down here) –
Remembered not the dank tarn of Auber,
　　Nor the ghoul-haunted woodland of Weir.

And now, as the night was senescent
　　And star-dials pointed to morn –
　　As the star-dials hinted of morn –
At the end of our path a liquescent
　　And nebulous lustre was born,
Out of which a miraculous crescent
　　Arose with a duplicate horn –
Astarte's bediamonded crescent
　　Distinct with its duplicate horn.

And I said – 'She is warmer than Dian:
　　She rolls through an ether of sighs –
　　She revels in a region of sighs:
She has seen that the tears are not dry on
　　These cheeks, where the worm never dies,
And has come past the stars of the Lion
　　To point us the path to the skies –
　　To the Lethean peace of the skies –
Come up, in despite of the Lion,
　　To shine on us with her bright eyes –
Come up through the lair of the Lion,
　　With love in her luminous eyes.'

But Psyche, uplifting her finger,
　　Said – 'Sadly this star I mistrust –
　　Her pallor I strangely mistrust: –
Oh, hasten! – oh, let us not linger!
　　Oh, fly! – let us fly! – for we must.'
In terror she spoke, letting sink her
　　Wings until they trailed in the dust –
In agony sobbed, letting sink her
　　Plumes till they trailed in the dust –
　　Till they sorrowfully trailed in the dust.

84

I replied – 'This is nothing but dreaming:
    Let us on by this tremulous light!
    Let us bathe in this crystalline light!
Its Sibyllic splendor is beaming
    With Hope and in Beauty to-night: –
    See! – it flickers up the sky through the night!
Ah, we safely may trust to its gleaming,
    And be sure it will lead us aright –
We safely may trust to a gleaming
    That cannot but guide us aright,
    Since it flickers up to Heaven through the night.'

Thus I pacified Psyche and kissed her,
    And tempted her out of her gloom –
    And conquered her scruples and gloom;
And we passed to the end of the vista,
    But were stopped by the door of a tomb –
    By the door of a legended tomb;
And I said – 'What is written, sweet sister,
    On the door of this legended tomb?'
    She replied – 'Ulalume – Ulalume –
    'Tis the vault of thy lost Ulalume!'

Then my heart it grew ashen and sober
    As the leaves that were crisped and sere –
    As the leaves that were withering and sere;
And I cried – 'It was surely October
    On *this* very night of last year
    That I journeyed – I journeyed down here –
    That I brought a dread burden down here –
    On this night of all nights in the year,
    Ah! what demon has tempted me here?
Well I know, now, this dim lake of Auber –
    This misty mid region of Weir –
Well I know, now, this dank tarn of Auber,
    This ghoul-haunted woodland of Weir.'

Annabel Lee

It was many and many a year ago,
    In a kingdom by the sea,
That a maiden there lived whom you may know
    By the name of ANNABEL LEE;
And this maiden she lived with no other thought
    Than to love and be loved by me.

I was a child and *she* was a child,
    In this kingdom by the sea:
But we loved with a love that was more than love –
    I and my ANNABEL LEE;
With a love that the winged seraphs of heaven
    Coveted her and me.

And this was the reason that, long ago,
    In this kingdom by the sea,
A wind blew out of a cloud, chilling
    My beautiful ANNABEL LEE;
So that her highborn kinsmen came
    And bore her away from me,
To shut her up in a sepulchre
    In this kingdom by the sea.

The angels, not half so happy in heaven,
    Went envying her and me –
Yes! – that was the reason (as all men know,
    In this kingdom by the sea)
That the wind came out of the cloud by night,
    Chilling and killing my ANNABEL LEE.

But our love it was stronger by far than the love
    Of those who were older than we –
    Of many far wiser than we –
And neither the angels in heaven above,
    Nor the demons down under the sea,
Can ever dissever my soul from the soul
    Of the beautiful ANNABEL LEE:

For the moon never beams, without bringing me dreams
    Of the beautiful ANNABEL LEE;
And the stars never rise, but I feel the bright eyes
    Of the beautiful ANNABEL LEE;
And so, all the night-tide, I lie down by the side
Of my darling, – my darling, – my life and my bride,
    In her sepulchre there by the sea,
    In her tomb by the side of the sea.

ESSAYS ON POETRY

The Poetic Principle

In speaking of the Poetic Principle, I have no design to be either thorough or profound. While discussing very much at random the essentiality of what we call Poetry, my principal purpose will be to cite for consideration some few of those minor English or American poems which best suit my own taste, or which, upon my own fancy, have left the most definite impression. By 'minor poems' I mean, of course, poems of little length. And here, in the beginning, permit me to say a few words in regard to a somewhat peculiar principle, which, whether rightfully or wrongfully, has always had its influence in my own critical estimate of the poem. I hold that a long poem does not exist. I maintain that the phrase, 'a long poem,' is simply a flat contradiction in terms.

I need scarcely observe that a poem deserves its title only inasmuch as it excites, by elevating the soul. The value of the poem is in the ratio of this elevating excitement. But all excitements are, through a psychal necessity, transient. That degree of excitement which would entitle a poem to be so called at all, cannot be sustained throughout a composition of any great length. After the lapse of half an hour, at the very utmost, it flags – fails – a revulsion ensues – and then the poem is, in effect, and in fact, no longer such.

There are, no doubt, many who have found difficulty in reconciling the critical dictum that the *Paradise Lost* is to be devoutly admired throughout, with the absolute impossibility of maintaining for it, during perusal, the amount of enthusiasm which that critical dictum would demand. This great work, in fact, is to be regarded as poetical only when, losing sight of that vital requisite in all works of Art, Unity, we view it merely as a series of minor poems. If, to preserve its Unity – its totality of effect or impression – we read it (as would be necessary) at a single sitting, the result is but a constant alternation of excitement and depression. After a passage of what we feel to be true poetry, there follows, inevitably, a passage of platitude which no critical pre-judgement can force us to admire; but if, upon completing the work, we read it again; omitting the first book – that is to say, commencing with the second – we shall be surprised at now finding that admirable which we before condemned – that damnable which we had previously so much admired. It follows from all this that the ultimate, aggregate, or absolute effect of even the best epic under the sun, is a nullity – and this is precisely the fact.

In regard to the *Iliad*, we have, if not positive proof, at least very good reason, for believing it intended as a series of lyrics; but, granting the epic intention, I can say only that the work is based in an imperfect sense of Art. The modern epic is, of the suppositional ancient model, but an inconsiderate and blindfold imitation. But the day of these artistic anomalies is over. If, at any time, any very long poems *were* popular in reality – which I doubt – it is at least clear that no very long poem will ever be popular again.

That the extent of a poetical work is, *ceteris paribus*, the measure of its merit, seems undoubtedly, when we thus state it, a proposition sufficiently absurd – yet we are indebted for it to the quarterly Reviews. Surely there can be nothing in mere *size* abstractly considered – there can be nothing in mere *bulk*, so far as a volume is concerned, which has so continuously elicited admiration from these saturnine pamphlets! A mountain, to be sure, by the mere sentiment of physical magnitude which it conveys, *does* impress us with a sense of the sublime – but no man is impressed after *this* fashion by the material grandeur of even *The Columbiad*. Even the Quarterlies have not instructed us to be so impressed by it. *As yet*, they have not *insisted* on our estimating Lamartine by the cubic foot, or Pollock by the pound – but what else are we to *infer* from their continual prating about 'sustained effort'? If, by 'sustained effort', any little gentleman has accomplished an epic, let us frankly commend him for the effort – if this indeed be a thing commendable – but let us forbear praising the epic on the effort's account. It is to be hoped that common sense, in the time to come, will prefer deciding upon a work of Art rather by the impression it makes – by the effect it produces – than by the time it took to impress the effect, or by the amount of 'sustained effort' which had been found necessary in effecting the impression. The fact is, that perseverance is one thing and genius quite another – nor can all the Quarterlies in Christendom confound them. By-and-by, this proposition, with many which I have been just urging, will be received as self-evident. In the meantime, by being generally condemned as falsities, they will not be essentially damaged as truths.

On the other hand, it is clear that a poem may be improperly brief. Undue brevity degenerates into mere epigrammatism. A *very* short poem, while now and then producing a brilliant or vivid, never produces a profound or enduring effect. There must be the steady pressing down of the stamp upon the wax. De Béranger has wrought innumerable things, pungent and spirit-stirring, but in general they have been too imponderous to stamp themselves deeply into the public attention, and thus, as so many feathers of fancy, have been blown aloft only to be whistled down the wind.

While the epic mania – while the idea that, to merit in poetry, prolixity is indispensable – has for some years past been gradually dying out of the public mind by mere dint of its own absurdity, we find it succeeded by a heresy too palpably false to be long tolerated, but one which, in the brief period it has already endured, may be said to have accomplished more in the corruption of our Poetical Literature than all its other enemies combined. I allude to the heresy of *The Didactic*. It has been assumed, tacitly and avowedly, directly and indirectly, that the ultimate object of all Poetry is Truth. Every poem, it is said, should inculcate a moral, and by this moral is the poetical merit of the work to be adjudged. We Americans especially have patronised this happy idea, and we Bostonians very especially have developed it in full. We have taken it into our heads that to write a poem simply for the poem's sake, and to acknowledge such to have been our design, would be to confess ourselves radically wanting in the true Poetic dignity and force: – but the simple fact is, that would we but permit ourselves to look into our own souls, we should immediately there discover that under the sun there neither exists nor *can* exist any work more thoroughly dignified, more supremely noble than this very poem, this poem *per se*, this poem which is a poem and nothing more, this poem written solely for the poem's sake.

With as deep a reverence for the True as ever inspired the bosom of man, I would nevertheless limit, in some measure, its modes of inculcation. I would limit to enforce them. I would not enfeeble them by dissipation. The demands of Truth are severe. She has no sympathy with the myrtles. All *that* which is so indispensable in Song, is precisely all *that* with which *she* has nothing whatever to do. It is but making her a flaunting paradox to wreathe her in gems and flowers. In enforcing a truth, we need severity rather than efflorescence of language. We must be simple, precise, terse. We must be cool, calm, unimpassioned. In a word, we must be in that mood which, as nearly as possible, is the exact converse of the poetical. *He* must be blind indeed who does not perceive the radical and chasmal differences between the truthful and the poetical modes of inculcation. He must be theory-mad beyond redemption who, in spite of these differences, shall still persist in attempting to reconcile the obstinate oils and waters of Poetry and Truth.

Dividing the world of mind into its three most immediately obvious distinctions, we have the Pure Intellect, Taste, and the Moral Sense. I place Taste in the middle because it is just this position which it occupies in the mind. It holds intimate relations with either extreme, but from the Moral Sense is separated by so faint a difference that Aristotle has not hesitated to place some of its operations among the virtues themselves. Nevertheless, we find the *offices* of the trio marked with a sufficient distinction. Just as the Intellect concerns itself with Truth, so Taste informs us of the Beautiful, while the Moral Sense is regardful of Duty. Of this latter, while Conscience teaches the obligation, and Reason the expediency, Taste contents herself with displaying the charms, waging war upon Vice solely on the ground of her deformity, her disproportion, her animosity to the fitting, to the appropriate, to the harmonious, in a word, to Beauty.

An immortal instinct deep within the spirit of man is thus plainly a sense of the Beautiful. This it is which administers to his delight in the manifold forms, and sounds, and odours, and sentiments, amid which he exists. And just as the lily is repeated in the lake, or the eyes of Amaryllis in the mirror, so is the mere oral or written repetition of these forms, and sounds, and colours, and odours, and sentiments, a duplicate source of delight. But this mere repetition is not poetry. He who shall simply sing, with however glowing enthusiasm, or with however vivid a truth of description, of the sights, and sounds, and odours, and colours, and sentiments, which greet *him* in common with all mankind – he, I say, has yet failed to prove his divine title. There is still a something in the distance which he has been unable to attain. We have still a thirst unquenchable, to allay which he has not shown us the crystal springs. This thirst belongs to the immortality of Man. It is at once a consequence and an indication of his perennial existence. It is the desire of the moth for the star. It is no mere appreciation of the Beauty before us, but a wild effort to reach the Beauty above. Inspired by an ecstatic prescience of the glories beyond the grave, we struggle by multiform combinations among the things and thoughts of Time to attain a portion of that Loveliness whose very elements perhaps appertain to eternity alone. And thus when by Poetry, or when by Music, the most entrancing of the Poetic moods, we find ourselves melted into tears, we weep then, not as the Abbaté Gravina supposes, through excess of pleasure, but through a certain, petulant, impatient sorrow at our inability to grasp *now*, wholly, here on earth, at once and for ever, those divine and rapturous joys of which *through* the poem, or *through* the music, we attain to but brief and indeterminate glimpses.

The struggle to apprehend the supernal Loveliness – this struggle, on the part of souls fittingly constituted – has given to the world all *that* which it (the world) has ever been enabled at once to understand and *to feel* as poetic.

The Poetic Sentiment, of course, may develope itself in various modes – in Painting, in Sculpture, in Architecture, in the Dance – very especially in Music – and very peculiarly, and with a wide field, in the composition of the Landscape Garden. Our present theme, however, has regard only to its manifestation in words. And here let me speak briefly on the topic of rhythm. Contenting myself with the certainty that Music, in its various modes of metre, rhythm, and rhyme, is of so vast a moment in Poetry as never to be wisely rejected – is so vitally important an adjunct, that he is simply silly who declines its assistance, I will not now pause to maintain its absolute essentiality. It is in Music perhaps that the soul most nearly attains the great end for which, when inspired by the Poetic Sentiment, it struggles – the creation of supernal Beauty. It *may* be, indeed, that here this sublime end is, now and then, attained in *fact*. We are often made to feel, with a shivering delight, that from an earthly harp are stricken notes which *cannot* have been unfamiliar to the angels. And thus there can be little doubt that in the union of Poetry with Music in its popular sense, we shall find the widest field for the Poetic development. The old Bards and Minnesingers had advantages which we do not possess – and Thomas Moore, singing his own songs, was, in the most legitimate manner, perfecting them as poems.

To recapitulate, then: – I would define, in brief, the Poetry of words as *The Rhythmical Creation of Beauty*. Its sole arbiter is Taste. With the Intellect or with the Conscience, it has only collateral relations. Unless incidentally, it has no concern whatever either with Duty or with Truth.

A few words, however, in explanation. *That* pleasure which is at once the most pure, the most elevating, and the most intense, is derived, I maintain, from the contemplation of the Beautiful. In the contemplation of Beauty we alone find it possible to attain that pleasurable elevation, or excitement *of the soul*, which we recognise as the Poetic Sentiment, and which is so easily distinguished from Truth, which is the satisfaction of the Reason, or from Passion, which is the excitement of the heart. I make Beauty, therefore – using the word as inclusive of the sublime – I make Beauty the province of the poem, simply because it is an obvious rule of Art that effects should be made to spring as directly as possible from their causes: – no one as yet having been weak enough to deny that the peculiar elevation in question is at least *most readily* attainable in the poem. It by no means follows, however, that the incitements of Passion, or the precepts of Duty, or even the lessons of Truth, may not be introduced into a poem, and with advantage; for they may subserve incidentally, in various ways, the general purposes of the work: – but the true artist will always contrive to tone them down in proper subjection to that *Beauty* which is the atmosphere and the real essence of the poem.

Thus, although in a very cursory and imperfect manner, I have endeavoured to convey to you my conception of the Poetic Principle. It has been my purpose to suggest that, while this Principle itself is strictly and simply the Human Aspiration for Supernal Beauty, the manifestation of the Principle is always found in *an elevating excitement of the soul*, quite independent of that passion which is the intoxication of the Heart, or of that truth which is the satisfaction of the Reason. For in regard to passion, alas! its tendency is to degrade rather than to elevate the Soul. Love, on the contrary – Love – the true, the divine Eros – the Uranian as distinguished from the Dionæan Venus – is unquestionably the purest and truest of all poetical themes. And in regard to Truth, if, to be sure, through the attainment of a truth we are led to perceive a harmony where none was apparent before, we experience at once the true poetical effect, but this effect is referable to the harmony alone, and not in the least degree to the truth which merely served to render the harmony manifest.

We shall reach, however, more immediately, a distinct conception of what the true Poetry is, by mere reference to a few of the simple elements which induce in the Poet himself the true poetical effect. He recognises the ambrosia which nourishes his soul in the bright orbs that shine in Heaven, in the volutes of the flower, in the clustering of low shrubberies, in the waving of the grain-fields, in the slanting of tall eastern trees, in the blue distance of mountains, in the grouping of clouds, in the twinkling of half-hidden brooks, in the gleaming of silver rivers, in the repose of sequestered lakes, in the star-mirroring depths of lonely wells. He perceives it in the songs of birds, in the harp of Æolus, in the sighing of the night-wind, in the repining voice of the forest, in the surf that complains to the shore, in the fresh breath of the woods, in the scent of the violet, in the voluptuous perfume of the hyacinth, in the suggestive odour that comes to him at eventide from far-distant undiscovered islands, over dim oceans, illimitable and unexplored. He owns it in all noble thoughts, in all unworldly motives, in all holy impulses, in all chivalrous, generous, and self-sacrificing deeds. He feels it in the beauty of woman, in the grace of her step, in the lustre of her eye, in the melody of her voice, in her soft laughter, in her sigh, in the harmony and rustling of her robes. He deeply feels it in her winning endearments, in her burning enthusiasms, in her gentle charities, in her meek and devotional endurances; but above all, ah, far above all, he kneels to it, he worships it in the faith, in the purity, in the strength, in the altogether divine majesty of her *love*.

The Rationale of Verse

The word 'Verse' is here used not in its strict or primitive sense, but as the term most convenient for expressing generally and without pedantry all that is involved in the consideration of rhythm, rhyme, metre, and versification.

There is, perhaps, no topic in polite literature which has been more pertinaciously discussed, and there is certainly not one about which so much inaccuracy, confusion, misconception, misrepresentation, mystification, and downright ignorance on all sides, can be fairly said to exist. Were the topic really difficult, or did it lie, even, in the cloudland of metaphysics, where the doubt-vapors may be made to assume any and every shape of the will or at the fancy of the gazer, we should have less reason to wonder at all this contradiction and perplexity; but in fact the subject is exceedingly simple; one tenth of it, possibly, may be called ethical; nine tenths, however, appertain to the mathematics; and the whole is included within the limits of the commonest common sense.

'But, if this is the case, how,' it will be asked, 'can so much misunderstanding have arisen? Is it conceivable that a thousand profound scholars, investigating so very simple a matter for centuries, have not been able to place it in the fullest light, at least, of which it is susceptible?' These queries, I confess, are not easily answered: – at all events a satisfactory reply to them might cost more trouble than would, if properly considered, the whole *vexata quæstio* to which they have reference. Nevertheless, there is little difficulty or danger in suggesting that the 'thousand profound scholars' *may* have failed, first, because they were scholars, secondly, because they were profound, and thirdly because they were a thousand – the impotency of the scholarship and profundity having been thus multiplied a thousand fold. I am serious in these suggestions; for, first again, there is something in 'scholarship' which seduces us into blind worship of Bacon's Idol of the Theatre – into irrational deference to antiquity; secondly, the proper 'profundity' is rarely profound – it is the nature of Truth in general, as of some ores in particular, to be richest when most superficial; thirdly, the clearest subject may be overclouded by mere superabundance of talk. In chemistry, the best way of separating two bodies is to add a third; in speculation, fact often agrees with fact and argument with argument, until an additional well-meaning fact or argument sets everything by the ears. In one case out of a hundred a point is excessively discussed because it is obscure; in the ninety-nine remaining it is obscure because excessively discussed. When a topic is thus circumstanced, the readiest mode of investigating it is to forget that any previous investigation has been attempted.

But, in fact, while much has been written on the Greek and Latin rhythms, and even on the Hebrew, little effort has been made at examining that of any of the modern tongues. As regards the English, comparatively nothing has been done. It may be said, indeed, that we are without a treatise on our own verse. In our ordinary grammars and in our works on rhetoric or prosody in general, may be found occasional chapters, it is true, which have the heading, 'Versification', but these are, in all instances, exceedingly meagre. They pretend to no analysis; they propose nothing like system; they make no attempt at even rule; every thing depends upon 'authority'. They are confined, in fact, to mere exemplification of the supposed varieties of English feet and English lines; – although in no work with which I am acquainted are these feet correctly given or these lines detailed in anything like their full extent. Yet what has been mentioned is all – if we except the occasional introduction to some pedagogue-ism, such as this, borrowed from the Greek Prosodies: – 'When a syllable is wanting, the verse is said to be catalectic; when the measure is exact, the line is acatalectic; when there is a redundant syllable it forms hypermeter.' Now whether a line be termed catalectic or acatalectic is, perhaps, a point of no vital importance; – it is even possible that the student may be able to decide, promptly, when the *a* should be employed and when omitted, yet be incognizant, at the same time, of *all* that is worth knowing in regard to the structure of verse.

A leading defect in each of our treatises, (if treatises they can be called,) is the confining the subject to mere *Versification*, while *Verse* in general, with the understanding given to the term in the heading of this paper, is the real question at issue. Nor am I aware of even one of our Grammars which so much as properly defines the word versification itself. 'Versification,' says a work now before me, of which the accuracy is far more than usual – the *English Grammar* of Goold Brown – 'Versification is the art of arranging words into lines of correspondent length, so as to produce harmony by the regular alternation of syllables differing in quantity.' The commencement of this definition might apply, indeed, to the *art* of versification, but not versification itself. Versification is not the art of arranging, &c., but the actual arranging – a distinction too obvious to need comment. The error here is identical with one which has been too long permitted to disgrace the initial page of every one of our school grammars. I allude to the definition of English Grammar itself. 'English Grammar,' it is said, 'is the art of speaking and writing the English language correctly.' This phraseology, or something essentially similar, is employed, I believe, by Bacon, Miller, Fisk, Greenleaf, Ingersoll, Kirkland, Cooper, Flint, Pue, Comly, and many others. These gentlemen, it is presumed, adopted it without examination from Murray, who derived it from Lily, (whose work was *'quam solam Regia Majestas in omnibus scholis docendam præcipit'*), and who appropriated it without acknowledgement, but with some unimportant modification, from the Latin Grammar of Leonicenus. It may be shown, however, that this definition, so complacently

97

received, is not, and cannot be, a proper definition of English Grammar. A definition is that which so describes its object as to distinguish it from all others: – it is no definition of any one thing if its terms are applicable to any one other. But if it be asked – 'What is the design – the end – the aim of English Grammar?' our obvious answer is, 'The art of speaking and writing the English language correctly': – that is to say, we must use the precise words employed as the definition of English Grammar itself. But the object to be obtained by any means is, assuredly, not the means. English Grammar and the end contemplated by English Grammar, are two matters sufficiently distinct; nor can the one be more reasonably regarded as the other than a fishing-hook as a fish. The definition, therefore, which is applicable in the latter instance, *cannot*, in the former, be true. Grammar in general is the analysis of language; English Grammar of the English.

But to return to Versification as defined in our extract above. 'It is the art,' says the extract, 'of arranging words into lines *of correspondent length.*' Not so: – a correspondence in the length of lines is by no means essential. Pindaric odes are, surely, instances of versification, yet these compositions are noted for extreme diversity in the length of their lines.

The arrangement is moreover said to be for the purpose of producing '*harmony* by the regular alternation,' &c. But *harmony* is not the sole aim – not even the principal one. In the construction of verse, *melody* should never be left out of view; yet this is a point which all our Prosodies have have most unaccountably forborne to touch. Reasoned rules on this topic should form a portion of all systems of rhythm.

'So as to produce harmony,' says the definition, 'by the *regular alternation,*' &c. A *regular* alternation, as described, forms no part of any principle of versification. The arrangement of spondees and dactyls, for example, in the Greek hexameter, is an arrangement which may be termed *at random*. At least it is arbitrary. Without interference with the line as a whole, a dactyl may be substituted for a spondee, or the converse, at any point other than the ultimate and penultimate feet, of which the former is always a spondee, the latter nearly always a dactyl. Here, it is clear, we have no '*regular* alternation of syllables differing in quantity'.

98

'So as to produce harmony,' proceeds the definition, 'by the regular alternation of *syllables differing in quantity*,' – in other words by the alternation of long and short syllables; for in rhythm all syllables are necessarily either short or long. But not only do I deny the necessity of any *regularity* in the succession of feet and, by consequence, of syllables, but dispute the essentiality of any *alternation*, regular or irregular, of syllables long and short. Our author, observe, is now engaged in a definition of versification in general, not of English versification in particular. But the Greek and Latin metres abound in the spondee and pyrrhic – the former consisting of two long syllables; the latter of two short; and there are innumerable instances of the immediate succession of many spondees and many pyrrhics.

Here is a passage from Silius Italicus:

Fallit te mensas inter quod credis inermem.
Tot bellis quæsita viro, tot cædibus armat
Majestas æterna ducem: si admoveris ora,
Cannas et Trebiam ante oculos Trasymenaque busta,
Et Pauli stare ingentem miraberis umbram.

Making the elisions demanded by the classic Prosodies, we should scan these Hexameters thus:

Fāllīt | tē mēn | sās īn | tēr qūod | crēdĭs ĭn | ērmēm |
Tōt bēl | līs qūæ | sītă vī | rō tōt | cædĭbŭs | ārmāt |
Mājēs | tās æ | tērnă dŭ | cēm s'ād | mōvĕrĭs | ōrā | ,
Cānnās | ēt Trĕbī' | ānt'ocŭ | lōs Trăsy | mēnăqŭe | būstā
Ēt Pāu | lī stā | r'īngēn | tēm mī | rābĕrīs | ūmbrām |

It will be seen that, in the first and last of these lines, we have only two short syllables in thirteen, with an uninterrupted succession of no less that *nine* long syllables. But how are we to reconcile all this with a definition of versification which describes it as 'the art of arranging words into lines of correspondent length so as to produce harmony by the *regular alternation of syllables differing in quantity*'?

It may be urged, however, that our prosodist's *intention* was to speak of the English metres alone, and that, by omitting all mention of the spondee and pyrrhic, he has virtually avowed their exclusion from our rhythms. A grammarian is never excusable on the ground of good intentions. We demand from him, if from any one, rigorous precision of style. But grant the design. Let us admit that our author, following the example of all authors on English Prosody, has, in defining versification at large, intended a definition merely of the English. All these prosodists, we will say, reject the spondee and pyrrhic. Still all admit the iambus, which consists of a short syllable followed by a long; the trochee, which is the converse of the iambus; the dactyl, formed of one long syllable followed by two short; and the anapæst – two short succeeded by a long. The spondee is improperly rejected, as I shall presently show. The pyrrhic is rightfully dismissed. Its existence in either ancient or modern rhythm is purely chimerical, and the insisting on so perplexing a nonentity as a foot of *two short* syllables, affords, perhaps, the best evidence of the gross irrationality and subservience to authority which characterize our Prosody. In the meantime the acknowledged dactyl and anapæst are enough to sustain my proposition about the 'alternation,' &c., without reference to feet which are assumed to exist in the Greek and Latin metres alone: for an anapæst and a dactyl may meet in the same line: when of course we shall have an uninterrupted succession of four short syllables. The meeting of these two feet, to be sure, is an accident not contemplated in the definition now discussed; for this definition, in demanding a 'regular alternation of syllables differing in quantity,' insists on a regular succession of similar *feet*. But here is an example:

Sīng tŏ mě | Isăbĕlle.

This is the opening line of a little ballad now before me, which proceeds in the same rhythm – a peculiarly beautiful one. More than all this: – English lines are often well composed, entirely, of a regular succession of syllables *all of the same quantity*: – the first lines, for instance, of the following quatrain by Arthur C. Coxe:

> *March! march! march!*
> Making sounds as they tread,
> Ho! ho! how they step,
> Going down to the dead!

The line italicised is formed of three cæsuras. The cæsura, of which I have much to say hereafter, is rejected by the English Prosodies and grossly misrepresented in the classic. It is a perfect foot – the most important in all verse – and consists of a single *long syllable; but the length of this syllable varies.*

It has thus been made evident that there is *not one* point of the definition in question which does not involve an error. And for anything more satisfactory or more intelligible we shall look in vain to any published treatise on the topic.

So general and so total a failure can be referred only to radical misconception. In fact the English Prosodists have blindly followed the pedants. These latter, like *les moutons de Panurge*, have been occupied in incessant tumbling into ditches, for the excellent reason that their leaders have so tumbled before. The *Iliad*, being taken as a starting point, was made to stand instead of Nature and common sense. Upon this poem, in place of facts and deduction from fact, or from natural law, were built systems of feet, metres, rhythms, rules, – rules that contradict each other every five minutes, and for nearly all of which there may be found twice as many exceptions as examples. If any one has a fancy to be thoroughly confounded – to see how far the infatuation of what is termed 'classical scholarship' can lead a book-worm in the manufacture of darkness out of sunshine, let him turn over, for a few moments, any of the German Greek Prosodies. The only thing clearly made out in them is a very magnificent contempt for Leibnitz's principle of 'a sufficient reason.'

To divert attention from the real matter in hand by any farther reference to these works, is unnecessary, and would be weak. I cannot call to mind, at this moment, one essential particular of information that is to be gleaned from them; and I will drop them here with merely this one observation: that, employing from among the numerous *'ancient'* feet the spondee, the trochee, the iambus, the anapæst, the dactyl, and the cæsura alone, I will engage to scan *correctly* any of the Horatian rhythms, or any true rhythm that human ingenuity can conceive. And this excess of chimerical feet is, perhaps, the very least of the scholastic supererogations. *Ex uno disce omnia.* The fact is that *Quantity* is a point in whose investigation the lumber of mere learning may be dispensed with, if ever in any. Its appreciation is universal. It appertains to no region, nor race, nor æra in especial. To melody and to harmony the Greeks hearkened with ears precisely similar to those which we employ for similar purposes at present; and I should not be condemned for heresy in asserting that a pendulum at Athens would have vibrated much after the same fashion as does a pendulum in the city of Penn.

Verse originates in the human enjoyment of equality, fitness. To this enjoyment, also, all the moods of verse – rhythm, metre, stanza, rhyme, alliteration, the *refrain*, and other analogous effects – are to be referred. As there are some readers who habitually confound rhythm and metre, it may be as well here to say that the former concerns the *character* of feet (that is, the arrangements of syllables) while the latter has to do with the *number* of these feet. Thus by 'a dactylic hexa*meter*' we imply a line or measure consisting of six of these dactyls.

To return to *equality*. Its idea embraces those of similarity, proportion, identity, repetition, and adaptation or fitness. It might not be very difficult to go even behind the idea of equality, and show both how and why it is that the human nature takes pleasure in it, but such an investigation would, for any purpose now in view, be supererogatory. It is sufficient that the *fact* is undeniable – the fact that man derives enjoyment from his perception of equality. Let us examine a crystal. We are at once interested by the equality between the sides and between the angles of one of its faces: the equality of the sides pleases us; that of the angles doubles the pleasure. On bringing to view a second face in all respects similar to the first, this pleasure seems to be squared; on bringing to view a third it appears to be cubed, and so on. I have no doubt, indeed, that the delight experienced, if measurable, would be found to have exact mathematical relations such as I suggest; that is to say, as far as a certainpoint, beyond which there would be a decrease in similar relations.

The perception of pleasure in the equality of *sounds* is the principle of *Music*. Unpractised ears can appreciate only simple equalities, such as are found in ballad airs. While comparing one simple sound with another they are too much occupied to be capable of comparing the equality subsisting between these two simple sounds, taken conjointly, and two other similar simple sounds taken conjointly. Practised ears, on the other hand, appreciate both equalities at the same instant – although it is absurd to suppose that both are *heard* at the same instant. One is heard and appreciated from itself: the other is heard by the memory; and the instant glides into and is confounded with the secondary, appreciation. Highly cultivated musical taste in this manner enjoys not only these double equalities, all appreciated at once, but takes pleasurable cognizance, through memory, of equalities the members of which occur at intervals so great that the uncultivated taste loses them altogether. That this latter can properly estimate or decide on the merits of what is called scientific music, is of course impossible. But scientific music has no claim to intrinsic excellence – it is fit for scientific ears alone. In its excess it is the triumph of the *physique* over the *morale* of music. The sentiment is overwhelmed by the sense. On the whole, the advocates of the simpler melody and harmony have infinitely the best of the argument; – although there has been very little of real argument on the subject.

In *verse*, which cannot be better designated than as an inferior or less capable Music, there is, happily, little chance for complexity. Its rigidly simple character not even Science – not even Pedantry can greatly pervert.

The rudiment of verse may, possibly, be found in the *spondee*. The very germ of a thought seeking satisfaction in equality of sound, would result in the construction of words of two syllables, equally accented. In corroboration of this idea we find that spondees most abound in the most ancient tongues. The second step we can easily suppose to be the comparison, that is to say, the collocation, of two spondees – of two words composed each of a spondee. The third step would be the juxta-position of three of these words. By this time the perception of monotone would induce farther consideration; and thus arises what Leigh Hunt so flounders in discussing under the title of 'The *Principle* of Variety in Uniformity'. Of course there is no principle in the case – nor in maintaining it. The 'Uniformity' is the principle: – the 'Variety' is but the principle's natural safeguard from self-destruction by excess of self. 'Uniformity', besides, is the very worst word that could have been chosen for the expression of the *general* idea at which it aims.

The perception of monotone having given rise to an attempt at its relief, the first thought in this new direction would be that of collating two or more words formed each of two syllables differently accented (that is to say, short and long) but having the same order in each word: – in other terms, of collating two or more iambuses, or two or more trochees. And here let me pause to assert that more pitiable nonsense has been written on the topic of *long* and *short* syllables than on any other subject under the sun. In general, a syllable is long or short, just as it is difficult or easy of enunciation. The *natural* long syllables are those encumbered – the *natural* short syllables are those *un*encumbered, with consonants; all the rest is mere artificiality and jargon. The Latin Prosodies have a rule that 'a vowel before two consonants is long.' This rule is deduced from 'authority' – that is, from the observation that vowels so circumstanced, in the ancient poems, are always in syllables long by the laws of scansion. The philosophy of the rule is untouched, and lies simply in the physical difficulty of giving voice to such syllables – of performing the lingual evolutions necessary for their utterance. Of course, it is not the *vowel* that is long, (although the rule says so) but the syllable of which the vowel is a part. It will be seen that the length of a syllable, depending on the facility or difficulty of its enunciation, must have great variation in various syllables; but for the purposes of verse we suppose a long syllable equal to two short ones: – and the natural deviation from this relativeness we correct in perusal. The more closely our long syllables approach this relation with our short ones, the better, *ceteris paribus*, will be our verse: but if the relation does not exist of itself, we force it by emphasis, which can, of course, make any syllable as long as desired; – or, by an effort we can pronounce with unnatural brevity a syllable that is naturally too long. *Accented* syllables are of course always long – but, where *un*encumbered with consonants, must be classed among the *unnaturally* long. Mere custom has declared that we shall accent them – that is to say, dwell upon them; but no inevitable lingual difficulty forces us to do so. In fine, every long syllable

104

must of its own accord occupy in its utterance, or must be *made* to occupy, precisely the time demanded for two short ones. The only exception to this rule is found in the cæsura – of which more anon.

The success of the experiment with the trochees or iambuses (the one would have suggested the other) must have led to a trial of dactyls or anapæsts – natural dactyls or anapæsts – dactylic or anapæstic *words*. And now some degree of complexity has been attained. There is an appreciation, first, of the equality between the several dactyls, or anapæsts, and secondly, of that between the long syllable and the two short conjointly. But here it may be said, that step after step would have been taken, in continuation of this routine, until all the feet of the Greek Prosodies became exhausted. Not so: – these remaining feet have no existence except in the brains of the scholiasts. It is needless to imagine men inventing these things, and folly to explain how and why they invented them, until it shall be first shown that they are actually invented. All other 'feet' than those which I have specified, are, if not impossible at first view, merely combinations of the specified; and, although this assertion is rigidly true, I will, to avoid misunderstanding, put it in a somewhat different shape. I will say, then, that at present I am aware of no *rhythm* – nor do I believe that any one can be constructed – which, in its last analysis, will not be found to consist altogether of the feet I have mentioned, either existing in their individual and obvious condition, or interwoven with each other in accordance with simple natural laws which I will endeavor to point out hereafter.

We have now gone so far as to suppose men constructing indefinite sequences of spondaic, iambic, trochaic, dactylic, or anapæstic words. In *extending* these sequences, they would be again arrested by the sense of monotone. A succession of spondees would *immediately* have displeased; one of iambuses or of trochees, on account of the variety included within the foot itself, would have taken longer to displease; one of dactyls or anapæsts, still longer: but even the last, if extended very far, must have become wearisome. The idea, first, of curtailing, and, secondly, of defining the length of, a sequence, would thus at once have arisen. Here then is the *line*, or verse proper.[1] The principle of equality being constantly at the bottom of the whole process, lines would naturally be made, in the first instance, equal in the number of their feet; in the second instance there would be variation in the mere number; one line would be twice as long as another; then one would be some less obvious multiple of another; then still less obvious proportions would be adopted: – nevertheless there would be *proportion*, that is to say, a phase of equality, still.

Lines being once introduced, the necessity of distinctly defining these lines *to the ear*, (as yet written verse does not exist,) would lead to a scrutiny of their capabilities *at their terminations*: – and now would spring up the idea of equality in sound between the final syllables – in other words, of *rhyme*. First, it would be used only in the iambic, anapæstic, and spondaic rhythms, (granting that the latter had not been thrown aside, long since, on account of its tameness;) because in these rhythms the concluding syllable being long, could best sustain the necessary protraction of the voice. No great while could elapse, however, before the effect, found pleasant as well as useful, would be applied to the two remaining rhythms. But as the chief force of rhyme must lie in the accented syllable, the attempt to create rhyme at all in these two remaining rhythms, the trochaic and dactylic, would necessarily result in double and triple rhymes, such as *beauty* with *duty* (trochaic,) and *beautiful* with *dutiful* (dactylic).

It must be observed that in suggesting these processes, I assign them no date; nor do I even insist upon their order. Rhyme is supposed to be of modern origin, and were this proved, my positions remain untouched. I may say, however, in passing, that several instances of rhyme occur in the *Clouds* of Aristophanes, and that the Roman poets occasionally employ it. There is an effective species of ancient rhyming which has never descended to the

[1] Verse, from the Latin *vertere*, to turn, is so called on account of the turning or re-commencement of the series of feet. Thus a verse, strictly speaking, is a line. In this sense, however, I have preferred using the latter word alone; employing the former in the general acceptation given it in the heading of this paper.

moderns; that in which the ultimate and penultimate syllables rhyme with each other. For example:

> Parturiunt montes et nascitur ridicu*lus mus*.

and again –

> Litoreis ingens inventa sub ilicib*us sus*.

The terminations of Hebrew verse, (as far as understood,) show no signs of rhyme; but what thinking person can doubt that it did actually exist? That men have so obstinately and blindly insisted, *in general*, even up to the present day, in confining rhyme to the *ends* of lines, when its effect is even better applicable elsewhere, intimates, in my opinion, the sense of some *necessity* in the connexion of the end with the rhyme – hints that the origin of rhyme lay in a necessity which connected it with the end – shows that neither mere accident nor mere fancy gave rise to the connexion – points, in a word, at the very necessity which I have suggested, (that of some mode of defining lines *to the ear*,) as the true origin of rhyme. Admit this, and we throw the origin far back in the night of Time – beyond the origin of written verse.

But, to resume. The amount of complexity I have now supposed to be attained is very considerable. Various systems of equalization are appreciated at once (or nearly so) in their respective values and in the value of each system with reference to all the others. As our present *ultimatum* of complexity, we have arrived at triple-rhymed, natural-dactylic lines, existing proportionally as well as equally with regard to other triple-rhymed, natural-dactylic lines. For example:

> Virginal Lilian, rigidly, humblily dutiful;
> Saintlily, lowlily,
> Thrillingly, holily
Beautiful!

Here we appreciate, first, the absolute equality between the long syllable of each dactyl and the two short conjointly; secondly, the absolute equality between each dactyl and any other dactyl – in other words, among all the dactyls; thirdly, the absolute equality between the two middle lines; fourthly, the absolute equality between the first line and the three others taken conjointly; fifthly, the absolute equality between the last two syllables of the respective words 'dutiful' and 'beautiful'; sixthly, the absolute equality between the two last syllables of the respective words 'lowlily' and 'holily'; seventhly, the proximate equality between the first syllable of 'dutiful' and the first syllable of 'beautiful'; eighthly, the proximate equality between the first syllable of 'lowlily' and that of 'holily'; ninthly, the proportional equality (that of five to one,) between the first line and each of its members, the dactyls; tenthly, the proportional equality (that of two to one,) between each of the middle lines and its members, the dactyls; eleventhly, the proportional equality between the first line and each of the two middle – that of five to two; twelfthly, the proportional equality between the first line and the last – that of five to one; thirteenthly, the proportional equality between each of the middle lines and the last – that of two to one; lastly, the proportional equality, as concerns number, between all the lines, taken collectively and any individual line – that of four to one.

The consideration of this last equality would give birth immediately to the idea of *stanza*[1] – that is to say, the insulation of lines into equal or obviously proportional masses. In its primitive, (which was also its best,) form, the stanza would most probably have had absolute unity. In other words, the removal of any one of its lines would have rendered it imperfect; as in the case above, where, if the last line, for example, be taken away, there is left no rhyme to the 'dutiful' of the first. Modern stanza is excessively loose – and where so, ineffective, as a matter of course.

Now, although in the deliberate written statement which I have here given of these various systems of equalities, there seems to be an infinity of complexity – so much that it is hard to conceive the mind taking cognizance of them all in the brief period occupied by the perusal or recital of the stanza – yet the difficulty is in fact apparent only when we will it to become so. Any one fond of mental experiment may satisfy himself, by trial, that, in listening to the lines, he does actually, (although with a seeming unconsciousness, on account of the rapid evolutions of

[1] A stanza is often vulgarly, and with gross impropriety, called a *verse*.

sensation,) recognize and instantaneously appreciate, (more or less intensely as his ear is cultivated,) each and all of the equalizations detailed. The pleasure received, or receivable, has very much such progressive increase, and in very nearly such mathematical relations, as those which I have suggested in the case of the crystal.

It will be observed that I speak of merely a proximate equality between the first syllable of 'dutiful' and that of 'beautiful'; and it may be asked why we cannot imagine the earliest rhymes to have had absolute instead of proximate equality of sound. But absolute equality would have involved the use of identical words; and it is the duplicate sameness or monotony – that of sense as well as that of sound – which would have caused these rhymes to be rejected in the very first instance.

The narrowness of the limits within which verse composed of natural feet alone, must necessarily have been confined, would have led, after a *very* brief interval, to the trial and immediate adoption of artificial feet – that is to say of feet *not* constituted each of single word, but two or even three words; or of parts of words. These feet would be intermingled with natural ones. For example:

ă brēath | căn māke | thĕm ās | ă breāth | hăs māde.

This is an iambic line in which each iambus is formed of two words. Again:

Thĕ ūn | ĭmā | gĭnā | blĕ mīght | ŏf Jōve. |

This is an iambic line in which the first foot is formed of a word and a part of a word; the second and third of parts taken from the body or interior of a word; the fourth of a part and a whole; the fifth of two complete words. There are no *natural* feet in either lines. Again:

Căn ĭt bĕ | fănciĕd thăt | Dēīty | ēvĕr vĭn | dīctĭvely |
Māde ĭn hĭs | īmăge ă | mānnĭkĭn | mērely tŏ | māddĕn ĭt? |

These are two dactylic lines in which we find natural feet, ('Deity', 'mannikin';) feet composed of two words ('fancied that', 'image a', 'merely to', 'madden it';) feet composed of three words ('can it be', 'made in his';) a foot composed of a part of a word ('dictively';) and a foot composed of a word and a part of a word ('ever vin').

And now, in our supposititious progress, we have gone so far as to exhaust all the *essentialities* of verse. What follows may, strictly speaking, be regarded as embellishment merely – but even in this embellishment, the rudimental sense of *equality* would have been the never-ceasing impulse. It would, for example, be simply in seeking farther administration to this sense that men would come, in time, to think of the *refrain*, or burden, where, at the closes of the several stanzas of a poem, one word or phrase is *repeated;* and of alliteration, in whose simplest form a consonant is *repeated* in the commencements of various words. This effect would be extended so as to embrace repetitions both of vowels and of consonants, in the bodies as well as in the beginnings of words; and, at a later period, would be made to infringe on the province of rhyme, by the introduction of general similarity of sound between whole feet occurring in the body of a line: – all of which modifications I have exemplified in the line above,

Made in his im*age a *mannikin* m*erely to *madden it.*

Farther cultivation would improve also the *refrain* by relieving its monotone in slightly varying the phrase at each repetition, or, (as I have attempted to do in 'The Raven',) in retaining the phrase and varying its application – although this latter point is not strictly a rhythmical effect *alone*. Finally, poets when fairly wearied with following precedent – following it the more closely the less they perceived it in company with Reason – would adventure so far as to indulge in positive rhyme at other points than the ends of lines. First, they would put it in the middle of the line; then at some point where the multiple would be less obvious; then, alarmed at their own audacity, they would undo all their work by cutting these lines in two. And here is the fruitful source of the infinity of 'short metre', by which modern poetry, if not distinguished, is at least disgraced. It would require a high degree, indeed, both of cultivation and of courage, on the part of any versifier, to enable him to place his rhymes – and let them remain – at unquestionably their best position, that of unusual and *unanticipated* intervals.

On account of the stupidity of some people, or, (if talent be a more respectable word,) on account of their talent for misconception – I think it necessary to add here, first, that I believe the 'processes' above detailed to be nearly if not accurately those which *did* occur in the gradual creation of what we now call verse; secondly, that, although I so believe, I yet urge neither the assumed fact nor my belief in it, as a part of the true propositions of this paper; thirdly, that in regard to the aim of this paper, it is of no consequence whether these processes did occur either in the order I have assigned them, or at all; my design being simply, in presenting a general type of what such processes *might* have been and *must* have resembled, to help *them*, the 'some people', to an easy understanding of what I have farther to say on the topic of Verse.

There is one point which, in my summary of the processes, I have purposely forborne to touch; because this point, being the most important of all, on account of the immensity of error usually involved in its consideration, would have led me into a series of detail inconsistent with the object of a summary.

Every reader of verse must have observed how seldom it happens that even any one line proceeds uniformly with a succession, such as I have supposed, of absolutely equal feet; that is to say, with a succession of iambuses only, or of trochees only, or of dactyls only, or of anapæsts only, or of spondees only. Even in the most musical lines we find the succession interrupted. The iambic pentameters of Pope, for example, will be found on examination, frequently varied by trochees in the beginning, or by (what seem to be) anapæsts in the body, of the line.

Ŏh thōu | whătē | vĕr tī | tlĕ pleāse | thĭne ĕār |
Dĕan Drā | piĕr Bĭck | ĕrstāff | ŏr Gūll | īvēr |
Whēthĕr | thŏu choōse | Cĕrvān | tĕs' sē | rĭoŭs āir |
Ŏr laūgh | ănd shāke | ĭn Rāb | ĕlaīs' eā | sy chaīr. |

Were any one weak enough to refer to the Prosodies for the solution of the difficulty here, he would find it *solved* as usual by a *rule*, stating the fact, (or what it, the rule, supposes to be the fact,) but without the slightest attempt at the *rationale*. 'By a *synæresis* of the two short syllables,' say the books, 'an anapæst may sometimes be employed for an iambus, or a dactyl for a

111

trochee.... In the beginning of a line a trochee is often used for an iambus.'

Blending is the plain English for *synæresis* – but there should be *no* blending; neither is an anapæst *ever* employed for an iambus, or a dactyl for a trochee. These feet differ in time; and *no* feet so differing can ever be legitimately used in the same line. An anapæst is equal to four short syllables – an iambus only to three. Dactyls and trochees hold the same relation. The principle of *equality*, in verse, admits, it is true, of variation at certain points, for the relief of monotone, as I have already shown, but the point of *time* is that point which, being the rudimental one, must never be tampered with at all.

To explain: – In farther efforts for the relief of monotone than those to which I have alluded in the summary, men soon came to see that there was no absolute necessity for adhering to the precise number of syllables, provided the time required for the whole foot was preserved inviolate. They saw, for instance, that in such a line as

Ŏr laūgh | ănd shāke | ĭn Rāb | ĕlaīs' eā | sy chaīr, |

the equalization of the three syllables *elaise ea* with the two syllables composing any of the other feet, could be readily affected by pronouncing the two syllables *elais* in double quick time. By pronouncing each of the syllables *e* and *lais* twice as rapidly as the syllable *sy*, or the syllable *in*, or any other short syllable, they could bring the two of them, taken together, to the length, that is to say to the time, of any one short syllable. This consideration enabled them to effect the agreeable variation of three syllables in place of the uniform two. And variation was the object – variation to the ear. What sense is there, then, in supposing this object rendered null by the *blending* of the two syllables so as to render them, in absolute effect, one? Of course, there must be *no* blending. Each syllable must be pronounced as distinctly as possible, (or the variation is lost,) but with twice the rapidity in which the ordinary short syllable is enunciated. That the syllables *elais ea* do not compose an *anapæst* is evident, and the signs (ăăā) of their accentuation are erroneous. The foot might be written thus (ạạạ) the inverted crescents expressing a double quick time; and might be called a bastard iambus.

112

Here is a trochaic line:

Sēe thĕ | dēlĭcăte | fōotĕd | rēindeĕr. |

The prosodies – that is to say the most considerate of them – would here decide that *'delicate* is a dactyl used in place of a trochee, and would refer to what they call their 'rule', for justification. Others, varying the stupidity, would insist upon a Procrustean adjustment thus (del'cate) an adjustment recommended to all such words as *silvery, murmuring,* etc., which, it is said, should be not only pronounced, but written *silv'ry, murm'ring,* and so on, whenever they find themselves in trochaic predicament. I have only to say that 'delicate', when circumstanced as above, is neither a dactyl nor a dactyl's equivalent; that I would suggest for it this (aa̯a = inverted) accentuation; that I think it as well to call it a bastard trochee; and that all words, at all events, should be written and pronounced *in full,* and as nearly as possible as nature intended them.

About eleven years ago, there appeared in *The American Monthly Magazine,* (then edited, I believe, by Mess. Hoffman and Benjamin,) a review of Mr Willis' Poems; the critic putting forth his strength, or his weakness, in an endeavor to show that the poet was either absurdly affected, or grossly ignorant of the laws of verse; the accusation being based altogether on the fact that Mr W. made occasional use of this very word 'delicate' and other similar words, in 'the Heroic measure which every one knew consisted of feet of two syllables.' Mr W. has often, for example, such lines as

> That binds him to a woman's *delicate* love –
> In the gay sunshine, *reverent* in the storm –
> With its *invisible* fingers my loose hair.

Here, of course, the feet *licate, love, verent in,* and *sible fin,* are bastard iambuses; are *not* anapæsts; and are *not* improperly used. Their employment, on the contrary, by Mr Willis, is but one of the innumerable instances he has given of keen sensibility in all those matters of taste which may be classed under the general head of *fanciful embellishment.*

It is also about eleven years ago, if I am not mistaken, since

113

Mr Horne, (of England,) the author of *Orion*, one of the noblest epics in any language, thought it necessary to preface his *Chaucer Modernized* by a very long and evidently very elaborate essay, of which the greater portion was occupied in a discussion of the seemingly anomalous foot of which we have been speaking. Mr Horne upholds Chaucer in its frequent use; maintains his superiority, *on account* of his so frequently using it, over all English versifiers; and, indignantly repelling the common idea of those who make verse on their fingers – that the superfluous syllable is a roughness and an error – very chivalrously makes battle for it as 'a grace'. That a grace it *is*, there can be no doubt; and what I complain of is, that the author of the most happily versified long poem in existence, should have been under the necessity of discussing this grace merely *as* a grace, through forty or fifty vague pages, solely because of his inability to show *how* and *why* it is a grace – by which showing the question would have been settled in an instant.

About the trochee used for an iambus, as we see in the beginning of the line,

> Whēthĕr thou choose Cervantes' serious air,

there is little that need be said. It brings me to the general proposition that, in all rhythms, the prevalent or distinctive feet may be varied at will, and nearly at random, by the *occasional* introduction of equivalent feet – that is to say, feet the sum of whose syllabic times is equal to the sum of the syllabic times of the distinctive feet. Thus the trochee, *whēthĕr*, is equal, in the sum of the times of its syllables, to the iambus, *thŏu choōse*, in the sum of the times of *its* syllables; each foot being, in time, equal to three short syllables. Good versifiers who happen to be, also, good poets, contrive to relieve the monotone of a series of feet, by the use of equivalent feet only at rare intervals, and at such points of their subject as seem in accordance with the *startling* character of the variation. Nothing of this care is seen in the line quoted above – although Pope has some fine instances of the duplicate effect. Where vehemence is to be strongly expressed, I am not sure that we should be wrong in venturing on *two consecutive* equivalent feet – although I cannot say that I have ever known the adventure

114

made, except in the following passage, which occurs in 'Al Aaraaf', a boyish poem, written by myself when a boy. I am referring to the sudden and rapid advent of a star.

> Dim was its little disk, and angel eyes
> Alone could see the phantom in the skies,
> Whĕn fīrst thĕ phāntŏm's cōurse wăs fōund tŏ bē
> *Hēadlŏng hīthĕr*ward o'er the starry sea.

In the 'general proposition' above, I speak of the *occasional* introduction of equivalent feet. It sometimes happens that unskilful versifiers, without knowing what they do, or why they do it, introduce so many 'variations' as to exceed in number the 'distinctive' feet; when the ear becomes at once balked by the *bouleversement* of the rhythm. Too many trochees, for example, inserted in an iambic rhythm, would convert the latter to a trochaic. I may note here, that, in all cases, the rhythm designed should be commenced and continued, *without* variation, until the ear has had full time to comprehend what *is* the rhythm. In violation of a rule so obviously founded in common sense, many even of our best poets, do not scruple to begin an iambic rhythm with a trochee, or the converse; and so on.

A somewhat less objectionable error, although still a decided one, is that of commencing a rhythm, not with a different equivalent foot, but with a 'bastard' foot of the rhythm intended. For example:

> Mānў ă | thōught wĭll | cōme tŏ | mēmŏry. |

Here *many a* is what I have explained to be a bastard trochee, and to be understood should be accented with inverted crescents. It is objectionable solely on account of its position as the *opening* foot of a trochaic rhythm. *Memory*, similarly accented, is also a bastard trochee, but *un*objectionable, although by no means demanded.

The farther illustration of this point will enable me to take an important step.

One of our finest poets, Mr Christopher Pearse Cranch, begins a very beautiful poem thus:

> Many are the thoughts that come to me
>   In my lonely musing;

115

And they drift so strange and swift
  There's no time for choosing
Which to follow; for to leave
  Any, seems a losing.

'A losing' to Mr Cranch, of course – but this *en passant*. It will be seen here that the intention is trochaic; – although we do *not* see this intention by the opening foot, as we should do – or even by the opening line. Reading the whole stanza, however, we perceive the trochaic rhythm as the general design, and so, after some reflection, we divide the first line thus:

Many are the | thōughts thăt | cōme tŏ | mē. |

Thus scanned, the line will seem musical. It *is* – highly so. And it is because there is no end to instances of just such lines of apparently incomprehensible music, that Coleridge thought proper to invent his nonsensical *system* of what he calls 'scanning by accents' – as if 'scanning by accents' were anything more than a phrase. Whenever 'Christabel' is really *not rough*, it can be as readily scanned by the true *laws* (not the supposititious *rules*) of verse, as can the simplest pentameter of Pope; and where it *is* rough (*passim*) these same laws will enable any one of common sense to show *why* it is rough and to point out, instantaneously, the remedy for the roughness.

A reads and re-reads a certain line, and pronounces it false in rhythm – unmusical. *B*, however, reads it *to A*, and *A* is at once struck with the perfection of the rhythm, and wonders at his dulness in not 'catching' it before. Henceforward he admits the line to be musical. *B*, triumphant, asserts, that, to be sure, the line is musical – for it is the work of Coleridge – and that it is *A* who is *not*; the fault being in *A*'s false reading. Now here *A* is right and *B* wrong. *That* rhythm is erroneous, (at some point or other more or less obvious,) which *any* ordinary reader *can*, without design, read improperly. It is the business of the poet so to construct his line that the intention *must* be caught *at once*. Even when these men have precisely the same understanding of a sentence, they differ and often widely, in their modes of enunciating it. Any one who has taken the trouble to examine the topic of emphasis, (by

116

which I here mean not *accent* of particular syllables, but the dwelling on entire words,) must have seen that men emphasize in the most singularly arbitrary manner. There are certain large classes of people, for example, who persist in emphasizing their monosyllables. Little uniformity of emphasis prevails; because the thing itself – the idea, emphasis, – is referable to no natural – at least, to no well comprehended and therefore uniform law. Beyond a very narrow and vague limit, the whole matter is conventionality. And if we differ in emphasis even when we agree in comprehension, how much more so in the former when in the latter too! Apart, however, from the consideration of natural disagreement, is it not clear that, by tripping here and mouthing there, any sequence of words may be twisted into any species of rhythm? But are we thence to deduce that all sequences of words are rhythmical in a rational understanding of the term? – for this is the deduction, precisely to which the *reductio ad absurdum* will, in the end, bring all the propositions of Coleridge. Out of a hundred readers of 'Christabel', fifty will be able to make nothing of its rhythm, while forty-nine of the remaining fifty will, with some ado, fancy they comprehend it, after the fourth or fifth perusal. The one out of the whole hundred who shall both comprehend and admire it at first sight – must be an unaccountably clever person – and I am far too modest to assume, for a moment, that that very clever person is myself.

In illustration of what is here advanced I cannot do better than quote a poem:

> Pease porridge hot – pease porridge cold –
> Pease porridge in the pot – nine days old.

Now those of my readers who have never *heard* this poem pronounced according to the nursery conventionality, will find its rhythm as obscure as an explanatory note; while those who *have* heard it, will divide it thus, declare it musical, and wonder how there can be any doubt about it.

> Pease | porridge | hot | pease | porridge | cold |
> Pease | porridge |in the | pot | nine | days | old. |

The chief thing in the way of this species of rhythm, is the necessity which it imposes upon the poet of travelling in constant

117

company with his compositions, so as to be ready at a moment's notice, to avail himself of a well understood poetical license – that of reading aloud one's own doggerel.

In Mr Cranch's line,

Many are the | thoughts that | come to | me, |

the general error of which I speak is, of course, very partially exemplified, and the purpose for which, chiefly, I cite it, lies yet further on in our topic.

The two divisions (*thoughts that*) and (*come to*) are ordinary trochees. Of the last division (*me*) we will talk hereafter. The first division (*many are the*) would be thus accented by the Greek Prosodies (mānȳ ăre thĕ) and would by called by them ἀστρόλογος. The Latin books would style the foot *Pæon Primus*, and both Greek and Latin would swear that it was composed of a trochee and what they term a pyrrhic – that is to say, a foot of two *short* syllables – a thing that *cannot be*, as I shall presently show.

But now, there is an obvious difficulty. The *astrologos*, according to the Prosodies' own showing, is equal to *five* short syllables, and the trochee to *three* – yet, in the line quoted, these two feet are equal. They occupy *precisely* the same time. In fact, the whole music of the line depends upon their being *made* to occupy the same time. The Prosodies then, have demonstrated what all mathematicians have stupidly failed in demonstrating – that three and five are one and the same thing.

After what I have already said, however, about the bastard trochee and the bastard iambus, no one can have any trouble in understanding that *many are the* is of similar character. It is merely a bolder variation than usual from the routine of trochees, and introduces to the bastard trochee one additional syllable. But this syllable is not *short*. That is, it is not short in the sense of '*short*' as applied to the final syllable of the ordinary trochee, where the word means merely *the half of long*.

In this case (that of the additional syllable) 'short', if used at all, must be used in the sense of *the sixth of long*. And all the three final syllables can be called *short* only with the same understanding of the term. The three together are equal only to the one short syllable (whose place they supply) of the ordinary trochee. It follows that there is no sense in thus (˘) accenting these syllables. We must devise for them some new character which shall denote the sixth of long. Let it be (͐) – the crescent placed with the curve to the left. The whole foot (māný aré thé) might be called a *quick trochee*.

We come now to the final division (*me*) of Mr Cranch's line. It is clear that this foot, short as it appears, is fully equal in time to each of the preceding. It is in fact the cæsura – the foot which, in the beginning of this paper, I called the most important in all verse. Its chief office is that of pause or termination; and here – at the end of a line – its use is easy, because there is no danger of misapprehending its value. We pause on it, by a seeming necessity, just so long as it has taken us to pronounce the preceding feet, whether iambuses, trochees, dactyls, or anapæsts. It is thus a *variable foot*, and, with some care, may be well introduced into the body of a line, as in a little poem of great beauty by Mrs Welby:

I have | a lit | tle step | s̃on | of on| ly three | years old. |

Here we dwell on the cæsura, *son*, just as long as it requires us to pronounce either of the preceding or succeeding iambuses. Its value, therefore, in this line, is that of three short syllables. In the following dactylic line its value is that of four short syllables.

Pale as a | lily was | Emily | G̃ray.

I have accented the cæsura with a (〰) by way of expressing this variability of value.

I observed, just now, that there could be no such foot as one of two short syllables. What we start from in the very beginning of all idea on the topic of verse, is quantity, *length*. Thus when we enunciate an independent syllable it is long, as a matter of course. If we enunciate two, dwelling on both equally, we express equality in the enumeration, or length, and have a right to call them two long syllables. If we dwell on one more than the other, we have also a right to call one short, because it is short in relation to the other. But if we dwell on both equally and with a tripping voice, saying to ourselves here are two short syllables, the query might well be asked of us – 'in relation to what are they short?' Shortness is but the negation of length. To say, then, that two

119

syllables, placed independently of any other syllable, are short, is merely to say that they have no positive length, or enunciation – in other words that they are no syllables – that they do not exist at all. And if, persisting, we add anything about their equality, where, x being equal to x, nothing is shown to be equal to zero. In a word, we can form no conception of a pyrrhic as of an independent foot. It is a mere chimera bred in the mad fancy of a pedant.

From what I have said about the equalization of the several feet of a *line*, it must not be deduced that any *necessity* for equality in time exists between the rhythm of *several* lines. A poem, or even a stanza, may begin with iambuses, in the first line, and proceed with anapæsts in the second, or even with the less accordant dactyls, as in the opening of quite a pretty specimen of verse by Miss Mary A. S. Aldrich:

> The wa | ter li| ly sleeps | in pride |
> Dōwn ĭn thĕ | dēpths ŏf thĕ | āzŭre | lake. |

Here *azure* is a spondee, equivalent to a dactyl; *lake* a cæsura.

I shall now best proceed in quoting the initial lines of Byron's 'Bride of Abydos':

> Know ye the land where the cypress and myrtle
>   Are emblems of deeds that are done in their clime –
> Where the rage of the vulture, the love of the turtle
>   Now melt into softness, now madden to crime?
> Know ye the land of the cedar and vine,
> Where the flowers ever blossom, the beams ever shine,
> And the light wings of Zephyr, oppressed with perfume,
> Wax faint o'er the gardens of Gul in their bloom?
> Where the citron and olive are fairest of fruit
> And the voice of the nightingale never is mute –
>   .   .   .   .
> Where the virgins are soft as the roses they twine,
> And all save the spirit of man is divine?
> 'Tis the land of the East – 'tis the clime of the Sun –
> Can he smile on such deeds as his children have done?
> Oh, wild as the accents of lovers' farewell
> Are the hearts that they bear and the tales that they tell.

Now the flow of these lines, (as times go,) is very sweet and musical. They have been often admired, and justly – as times go – that is to say, it is a rare thing to find better versification of its kind. And where verse is pleasant to the ear, it is silly to find fault with it because it refuses to be scanned. Yet I have heard men, professing to be scholars, who made no scruple of abusing these lines of Byron's on the ground that they were musical in spite of *all law*. Other gentlemen, *not* scholars, abused 'all law' for the same reason: – and it occurred neither to the one party nor to the other that the law about which they were disputing might possibly be no law at all – an ass of a law in the skin of a lion.

The Grammars said something about dactylic lines, and it was easily seen that *these* lines were at least meant for dactylic. The first one was, therefore, thus divided:

Knōw yĕ thĕ | lānd whĕre thĕ | cyprĕss ănd | mȳrtlĕ. |

The concluding foot was a mystery; but the Prosodies said something about the dactylic 'measure' calling now and then for a double rhyme, without exactly perceiving what a double rhyme had to do with the question of an irregular foot. Quitting the first line, the second was thus scanned:

Arē ĕmblĕms | ōf deĕds thăt | āre dōne īn | their clīme. |

It was immediately seen, however, that *this* would not do: – it was at war with the whole emphasis of the reading. It could not be supposed that Byron, or any one in his senses, intended to place stress upon such monosyllables as 'are', 'of', and 'their', nor could 'their clime', collated with 'to crime', in the corresponding line below, be fairly twisted into anything like a 'double rhyme', so as to bring everything within the category of the Grammars. But farther these Grammars spoke not. The inquirers, therefore, in spite of their sense of harmony in the lines, when considered without reference to scansion, fell back upon the idea that the 'Are' was a blunder – an excess for which the poet should be sent to Coventry – and, striking it out, they scanned the remainder of the line as follows:

— ēmblĕms ŏf | deēds thăt ăre | dōne īn their | clīme. |

This answered pretty well; but the Grammars admitted no such foot of one syllable; and besides the rhythm was dactylic. In despair, the books are well searched, however, and at last the investigators are gratified by a full solution of the riddle in the profound 'Observation' quoted in the beginning of this article: – 'When a syllable is wanting, the verse is said to be catalectic; when the measure is exact, the line is acatalectic; when there is a redundant syllable it forms hypermeter.' This is enough. The anomalous line is pronounced to be catalectic at the head and to form hypermeter at the tail: – and so on, and so on; it being soon discovered that nearly all the remaining lines are in a similar predicament, and that what flows so smoothly to the ear, although so roughly to the eye, is, after all, a mere jumble of catalectism, acatalectism, and hypermeter – not to say worse.

Now, had this court of inquiry been in possession of even the shadow of the *philosophy* of Verse, they would have had no trouble in reconciling this oil and water of the eye and ear, by merely scanning the passage without reference to lines, and, continuously, thus:

> Know ye the | land where the | cypress and | myrtle Are | emblems of | deeds that are | done in their | clime Where the | rage of the | vulture the | love of the | turtle Now | melt into | softness now | madden to | *crime* | Know ye the | land of the | cedar and | vine Where the | flowers ever | blossom the | beams ever | shine Where the | light wings of | Zephyr op | pressed by per | *fume Wax* | faint o'er the | gardens of | Gul in their | bloom Where the | citron and | olive are | fairest of | fruit And the | voice of the | nightingale | never is | mute Where the | virgins are | soft as the | roses they | *twine And* | all save the | spirit of | man is di | vine 'Tis the | land of the | East 'tis the | clime of the | Sun Can he | smile on such | deeds as his | children have | *done Oh* | wild as the | accent of | lovers' fare | well Are the | hearts that they | bear and the | tales that they | *tell*.

Here 'crime' and 'tell' (italicized) are cæsuras, each having the value of a dactyl, four short syllables; while 'fume Wax', 'twine and', and 'done Oh', are spondees which, of course, being composed of two long syllables, are also equal to four short, and are

122

the dactyl's natural equivalent. The nicety of Byron's ear has led him into a succession of feet which, with two trivial exceptions as regards melody, are absolutely accurate – a very rare occurrence this in dactylic or anapæstic rhythms. The exceptions are found in the spondee '*twine And*', and the dactyl, '*smile on such*'. Both feet are false in point of melody. In '*twine And*', to make out the rhythm, we must force '*And*' into a length which it will not naturally bear. We are called on to sacrifice either the proper length of the syllable as demanded by its position as a member of a spondee, or the customary accentuation of the word in conversation. There is no hesitation, and should be none. We at once give up the sound for the sense; and the rhythm is imperfect. In this instance it is *very* slightly so; – not one person in ten thousand could, by ear, detect the inaccuracy. But the *perfection* of verse, as regards melody, consists in its *never* demanding any such sacrifice as is here demanded. The rhythmical must agree, *thoroughly*, with the reading, flow. This perfection has in no instance been attained – but is unquestionably attainable. '*Smile on such*', the dactyl, is incorrect, because '*such*', from the character of the two consonants *ch*, cannot *easily* be enunciated in the ordinary time of a short syllable, which its position declares that it is. Almost every reader will be able to appreciate the slight difficulty here; and yet the error is by no means so important as that of the '*And*' in the spondee. By dexterity we *may* pronounce '*such*' in the true time; but the attempt to remedy the rhythmical deficiency of the *And* by drawing it out, merely aggravates the offence against natural enunciation, by directing attention to the offence.

My main object, however, in quoting these lines, is to show that, in spite of the Prosodies, the length of a line is entirely an arbitrary matter. We might divide the commencement of Byron's poem thus:

Know ye the | land where the. |

or thus:

Know ye the | land where the | cypress and. |

or thus:

Know ye the | land where the | cypress and | myrtle are. |

or thus:

> Know ye the | land where the | cypress and | myrtle are |
> emblems of. |

In short, we may give it any division we please, and the lines will
be good – provided we have at least *two* feet in a line. As in
mathematics two units are required to form number, so rhythm,
(from the Greek ἀριθμος, number,) demands for its formation at
least two feet. Beyond doubt, we often see such lines as

> Know ye the –
> Land where the –

lines of one foot; and our Prosodies admit such; but with impropriety;
for common sense would dictate that every so obvious division
of a poem as is made by a line, should include within itself all
that is necessary for its own comprehension; but in a line of one
foot we can have no appreciation of *rhythm*, which depends upon
the equality between *two* or more pulsations. The false lines, consisting
sometimes of a single cæsura, which are seen in mock Pindaric
odes, are of course 'rhythmical' only in connection with
some other line; and it is this want of independent rhythm which
adapts them to the purposes of burlesque alone. Their effect is
that of incongruity (the principle of mirth); for they include the
blankness of prose amid the harmony of verse.

My second object in quoting Byron's lines, was that of showing
how absurd it often is to cite a single line from amid the body of
a poem, for the purpose of instancing the perfection or imperfection
of the line's rhythm. Were we to see by itself

> Know ye the land where the cypress and myrtle,

we might justly condemn it as defective in the final foot, which is
equal to only three, instead of being equal to four, short syllables.

In the foot (*flowers ever*) we shall find a further exemplification
of the principle of the bastard iambus, bastard trochee, and quick
trochee, as I have been at some pains in describing these feet
above. All the Prosodies on English verse would insist upon
making an elision in 'flowers', thus (flow'rs,) but this is nonsense.
In the quick trochee (mānȳ ăre thĕ) occurring in Mr Cranch's

trochaic line, we had to equalize the time of the three syllables (*ny,* *are, the,*) to that of the one *short* syllable whose position they usurp. Accordingly each of these syllables is equal to the third of a short syllable, that is to say, the *sixth of a long*. But in Byron's *dactylic* rhythm, we have to equalize the time of the three syllables (*ers, ev, er,*) to that of the one *long* syllable whose position they usurp or, (which is the same thing,) of the *two short*. Therefore the value of each of the syllables (*ers, ev,* and *er,*) is the *third of a long*. We enunciate them with only half the rapidity we employ in enunciating the three final syllables of the quick trochee – which latter is a rare foot. The '*flowers ever*', on the contrary, is as common in the dactylic rhythm as is the *bastard* trochee in the trochaic, or the bastard iambus in the iambic. We may as well accent it with the curve of the crescent to the right, and call it a *bastard dactyl*. A *bastard anapæst*, whose nature I now need to be at no trouble in explaining, will of course occur, now and then, in an anapæstic rhythm.

In order to avoid any chance of that condition which is apt to be introduced in an essay of this kind by too sudden and radical an alteration of the conventionalities to which the reader has been accustomed, I have thought it right to suggest for the accent marks of the bastard trochee, bastard iambus, etc., etc., certain characters which, in merely varying the direction of the ordinary short accent (˘) should imply, what is the fact, that the feet themselves are not *new* feet, in any proper sense, but simply modifications of the feet, respectively, from which they derive their names. Thus a bastard iambus is, in its essentiality, that is to say, in its time, an iambus. The variation lies only in the *distribution* of this time. The time, for example, occupied by the one short (or *half of long*) syllable, in the ordinary iambus, is, in the bastard, spread equally over two syllables, which are accordingly the *fourth of long*.

But this fact – the fact of the essentiality, or whole time, of the foot being unchanged, is now so fully before the reader, that I may venture to propose, finally, an accentuation which shall answer the real purpose – that is to say, what should be the real purpose of all accentuation – the purpose of expressing to the eye the exact relative value of every syllable employed in Verse.

125

I have already shown that enunciation, or *length*, is the point from which we start. In other words, we begin with a *long syllable*. This then is our unit; and there will be no need of accenting it at all. An unaccented syllable, in a system of accentuation, is to be regarded always as a long syllable. Thus a spondee would be without accent. In an iambus, the first syllable being 'short', or the *half* of long, should be accented with a small 2, placed *beneath* the syllable; the last syllable, being long, should be unaccented; – the whole would be thus (contr$\underset{2}{o}$l). In a trochee, these accents would be merely conversed, thus (m$\underset{2}{a}$nly). In a dactyl, each of the two final syllables, being the half of long, should, also, be accented with a small 2 beneath the syllable; and, the first syllable left unaccented, the whole would be thus (happin$\underset{2}{e}$ $\underset{2}{s}$s). In an anapæst we should converse the dactyl thus, (in th$\underset{2}{e}$ l$\underset{2}{a}$nd). In the bastard dactyl, each of the three concluding syllables being the *third* of long, should be accented with a small 3 beneath the syllable and the whole foot would stand thus, (flow$\underset{3}{e}$rs $\underset{3}{e}$v$\underset{3}{e}$r). In the bastard anapæst we should converse the bastard dactyl thus, (in $\underset{3}{t}$h$\underset{3}{e}$ reb$\underset{3}{o}$und). In the bastard iambus, each of the two initial syllables, being the fourth of long, should be accented, below with a small 4; the whole foot would be thus, (in th$\underset{4}{e}$ r$\underset{4}{a}$in). In the bastard trochee, we should converse the bastard iambus thus, (m$\underset{4}{a}$ny $\underset{4}{a}$). In the quick trochee, each of the three concluding syllables, being the *sixth* of long, should be accented, below, with a small 6; the whole foot would be thus, (m$\underset{6}{a}$ny $\underset{6}{a}$re th$\underset{6}{e}$). The quick iambus is not yet created, and most probably never will be, for it will be excessively useless, awkward, and liable to misconception – as I have already shown that even the quick trochee is: – but, should it appear, we must accent it by conversing the quick trochee. The cæsura, being variable in length, but always *longer than 'long'*, should be accented, *above*, with a number expressing the length, or value, of the distinctive foot of the rhythm in which it occurs. Thus a cæsura, occurring in a spondaic rhythm, would be accented with a small 2 above the syllable, or rather, foot. Occurring in a dactylic or anapæstic rhythm, we also accent it

126

with the 2, above the foot. Occurring in an iambic rhythm, however, it must be accented, above, with 1½; for this is the relative value of the iambus. Occurring in the trochaic rhythm, we give it, of course, the same accentuation. For the complex 1½, however, it would be advisable to substitute the simpler expression ³⁄₂ which amounts to the same thing.

In this system of accentuation Mr Cranch's lines, quoted above, would thus be written:

$$\frac{3}{2}$$
Many are the | thoughts that | come to | me
$$_6 \quad _6 \quad _6 \qquad\qquad _2 \qquad _2$$
In my | lonely | musing, |
$$_2 \quad\quad _2 \quad\quad _2$$

$$\frac{3}{2}$$
And they | drift so | strange and | swift
$$_2 \qquad _2 \qquad\quad _2$$
There's no | time for | choosing |
$$_2 \qquad\quad _2 \qquad\quad _2$$
$$\frac{3}{2}$$
Which to | follow | for to | leave
$$_2 \qquad _2 \qquad _2$$
Any, | seems a | losing. |
$$_2 \qquad _2 \qquad _2$$

In the ordinary system the accentuation would be thus:

Mānÿ arĕ thĕ | thōughts thăt | cōme tŏ | mē
Īn mÿ | lōnelÿ | mŭsīng, |
Ānd thĕy | drīft sŏ | strānge ănd | swīft |
Thēre's nŏ | tīme fŏr | choōsīng |
Whīch tŏ | fōllŏw, | fōr tŏ | lēave
Āny, | seēms ă | lōsīng. |

It must be observed, here, that I do not grant this to be the 'ordinary' *scansion*. On the contrary, I never yet met the man who had the faintest comprehension of the true scanning of these lines, or of such as these. But granting this to be the mode in which our Prosodies would divide the feet, they would accentuate the syllables as just above.

Now, let any reasonable person compare the two modes. The first advantage seen in my mode is that of simplicity – of time, labor, and ink saved. Counting the fractions as *two* accents, even, there will be found only *twenty-six* accents to the stanza. In the common accentuation there are *forty-one*. But admit that all this is a trifle, which it is *not*, and let us proceed to points of importance. Does the common accentuation express the truth, in particular, in general, or in any regard? Is it consistent with itself? Does it convey either to the ignorant or to the scholar a just conception of the rhythm of the lines? Each of these questions must be answered in the negative. The crescents, being precisely similar, must be understood as expressing, all of them, one and the same thing; and so all Prosodies have always understood them and wished them to be understood. They express, indeed, 'short' – but this word has all kinds of meanings. It serves to represent (the reader is left to guess *when*) sometimes the half, sometimes the third, sometimes the fourth, sometimes the sixth, of 'long' – while 'long' itself, in the books, is left undefined and undescribed. On the other hand, the horizontal accent, it may be said, expresses sufficiently well, and unvaryingly, the syllables which are meant to be long. It does nothing of the kind. This horizontal accent is placed over the cæsura (wherever, as in the Latin Prosodies, the cæsura is recognized) as well as over the ordinary long syllable, and implies anything and everything, just as the crescent. But grant that it does express the ordinary long syllables, (leaving the cæsura out of question,) have I not given the identical expression, by not employing any expression at all? In a word, while the Prosodies, with a certain number of accents, express *precisely nothing whatever*, I, with scarcely half the number, have expressed everything which, in a system of accentuation, demands expression. In glancing at my mode in the lines of Mr Cranch, it will be seen that it conveys not only the exact relation of the syllables and feet, among themselves, in those particular lines, but their precise value in relation to any other existing or conceivable feet or syllables, in any existing or conceivable system of rhythm.

The object of what we call *scansion* is the distinct marking of the rhythmical flow. Scansion with accents or perpendicular lines between the feet – that is to say scansion *by* the voice only – is scansion *to* the ear only; and all very good in its way. The written scansion addresses the ear through the eye. In either case the object is the distinct marking of the rhythmical, musical, or reading flow. There *can* be not other object and there is none. Of course, then, the scansion and the reading flow should go hand in hand. The former must agree with the latter. The former represents and expresses the latter; and is good or bad as it truly or falsely represents and expresses it. If by the written scansion of a line we are not enabled to perceive any rhythm or music in the line, then either the line is unrhythmical or the scansion false. Apply all this to the English lines which we have quoted, at various points, in the course of this article. It will be found that the scansion exactly conveys the rhythm, and thus thoroughly fulfils the only purpose for which scansion is required.

But let the scansion *of the schools* be applied to the Greek and Latin verse, and what results do we find? – that the verse is one thing and the scansion quite another. The ancient verse, *read* aloud, is in general musical, and occasionally *very* musical. *Scanned* by the Prosodial rules we can, for the most part, make nothing of it whatever. In the case of the English verse, the more emphatically we dwell on the divisions between the feet, the more distinct is our perception of the kind of rhythm intended. In the case of the Greek and Latin, the more we dwell the *less* distinct is this perception. To make this clear by an example:

> Mæcenas, atavis edite regibus,
> O, et præsidium et dulce decus meum,
> Sunt quos curriculo pulverem Olympicum
> Collegisse juvat, metaque fervidis
> Evitata rotis, palmaque nobilis
> Terrarum dominos evehit ad Deos.

Now in *reading* these lines, there is scarcely one person in a thousand who, if even ignorant of Latin, will not immediately feel and appreciate their flow – their music. A prosodist, however, informs the public that the *scansion* runs thus:

> Mæce | nas ata | vis | edite | regibus |
> O, et | præsidi' | et | dulce de | cus meum |
> Sunt quos | curricu | lo | pulver' O | lympicum |
> Colle | gisse ju | vat | metaque | fervidis |
> Evi | tata ro | tis | palmaque | nobilis |
> Terra | rum domi | nos | evehit | ad Deos. |

129

Now I do not deny that we get a *certain sort* of music from the lines if we read them according to this scansion, but I wish to call attention to the fact that this scansion and the certain sort of music which grows out of it, are entirely at war not only with the reading flow which any ordinary person would naturally give the lines, but with the reading flow universally given them, and never denied them, by even the most obstinate and stolid of scholars.

And now these questions are forced upon us – 'Why exists this discrepancy between the modern verse with its scansion, and the ancient verse with its scansion?' – 'Why, in the former case, are there agreement and representation, while in the latter there is neither the one or the other?' or, to come to the point, – 'How are we to reconcile the ancient verse with the scholastic scansion of it?' This absolutely necessary conciliation – shall we bring it about by supposing the scholastic scansion wrong because the ancient verse is right, or by maintaining that the ancient verse is wrong because the scholastic scansion is not to be gainsaid?

Were we to adopt the latter mode of arranging the difficulty, we might, in some measure, at least simplify the expression of the arrangement by putting it thus – Because the pedants have no eyes, therefore the old poets had no ears.

'But,' say the gentlemen without the eyes, 'the scholastic scansion, although certainly not handed down to us in form from the old poets themselves (the gentlemen without the ears,) is nevertheless deduced from certain facts which are supplied us by careful observation of the old poems.'

And let us illustrate this strong position by an example from an American poet – who must be a poet of some eminence, or he will not answer the purpose. Let us take Mr Alfred B. Street. I remember these two lines of his:

> His sinuous path, by blazes, wound
> Among trunks grouped in myriads round.

With the *sense* of these lines I have nothing to do. When a poet is in a 'fine phrenzy', he may as well imagine a large forest as a small one – and 'by blazes!' is *not* intended for an oath. My concern is with the rhythm, which is iambic.

130

Now let us suppose that, a thousand years hence, when the 'American langugage' is dead, a learned prodist should be deducing from 'careful observation' of our best poets, a system of scansion for our poetry. And let us suppose that this prosodist had so little dependence in the generality and immutability of the laws of Nature, as to assume in the outset, that, because we lived a thousand years before his time and made use of steam-engines instead of mesmeric balloons, we must therefore have had a *very* singular fashion of mouthing our vowels, and altogether of hudsonizing our verse. And let us suppose that with these and other fundamental propositions carefully put away in his brain, he should arrive at the line, –

Among | trunks grouped | in my | riads round.

Finding it an obviously iambic rhythm, he would divide it as above, and observing that 'trunks' made the first member of an iambus, he would call it short, as Mr Street intended it to be. Now farther: – if instead of admitting the possibility that Mr Street, (who by that time would be called Street simply, just as we say Homer) – that Mr Street might have been in the habit of writing carelessly, as the poets of the prosodist's own era did, and as all poets will do (on account of being geniuses) – instead of admitting this, suppose the learned scholar should make a 'rule' and put it in a book, to the effect that, in the American verse, the vowel *u, when found imbedded among nine consonants* was *short*: what, under such circumstances, would the sensible people of the scholar's day have a right not only to think, but to say of that scholar? – why, that he was 'a fool, – by blazes!'

I have put an extreme case, but it strikes at the root of the error. The 'rules' are grounded in 'authority' – and this 'authority' – can any one tell us what it means? or can any one suggest anything that it may *not* mean? Is it not clear that the 'scholar' above referred to, might as readily have deduced from authority a totally false system as a partially true one? To deduce from authority a consistent prosody of the ancient metres would indeed have been within the limits of the barest possibility; and the task has *not* been accomplished, for the reason that it demands a species of ratiocination altogether out of keeping with the brain of a

bookworm. A rigid scrutiny will show that the very few 'rules'
which have not as many exceptions as examples, are those which
have, by accident, their true bases not in authority, but in the
omniprevalent laws of syllabification; such, for example, as the
rule which declares a vowel before two consonants to be long.

In a word, the gross confusion and antagonism of the scholastic
prosody, as well as its marked inapplicability to the reading flow
of the rhythms it pretends to illustrate, are attributable, first, to
the utter absence of natural principle as a guide in the investiga-
tions which have been undertaken by inadequate men; and sec-
ondly, to the neglect of the obvious consideration that the ancient
poems, which have been the *criteria* throughout, were the work
of men who must have written as loosely, and with as little defini-
tive system, as ourselves.

Were Horace alive to-day, he would divide for us his first Ode
thus, and 'make great eyes' when assured by the prosodists that
he had no business to make any such division!

> Mæcenas | atavis | edite | regibus |
> $_2$ $_2$ $_2$ $_2$ $_2$ $_2$ $_2$ $_2$
> O et præ | sidium et | dulce de | cus meum |
> $_2$ $_2$ $_3$ $_3$ $_3$ $_2$ $_2$ $_2$ $_2$
> Sunt quos cur | riculo | pulverem O | lympicum |
> $_2$ $_2$ $_2$ $_2$ $_2$ $_3$ $_3$ $_2$ $_2$
> Collegisse | juvat metaque | fervidis |
> $_3$ $_3$ $_3$ $_2$ $_2$ $_2$ $_2$
> Evitata | rotis palmaque | nobilis |
> $_3$ $_3$ $_3$ $_2$ $_2$ $_2$ $_2$
> Terrarum | dominos | evehit | ad Deos. |
> $_2$ $_2$ $_2$ $_2$ $_2$ $_2$ $_2$

Read by this scansion, the flow is preserved; and the more we
dwell on the divisions, the more the intended rhythm becomes
apparent. Moreover, the feet have all the same time; while, in the
scholastic scansion, trochees – admitted trochees – are absurdly
employed as equivalents to spondees and dactyls. The books
declare, for instance, that *Colle*, which begins the fourth line, is a
trochee, and seem to be gloriously unconscious that to put a
trochee in opposition with a longer foot, is to violate the inviol-
able principle of all music, *time*.

It will be said, however, by 'some people', that I have no busi-
ness to make a dactyl out of such obviously long syllables as *sunt*,
quos, cur. Certainly I have no business to do so. I *never* do so. And
Horace should not have done so. But he did. Mr Bryant and Mr

132

Longfellow do the same thing every day. And merely because these gentlemen, now and then, forget themselves in this way, it would be hard if some future prosodist should insist upon twisting the 'Thanatopsis', or the 'Spanish Student', into a jumble of trochees, spondees, and dactyls.

It may be said, also, by some other people, that in the word *decus*, I have succeeded no better than the books, in making the scansional agree with the reading flow; and that *decus* was not pronounced de*cus*. I reply, that there can be no doubt of the word having been pronounced, in this case, de*cus*. It must be observed, that the Latin inflection, or variation of a word in its terminating syllables, caused the Romans – *must* have caused them, to pay greater attention to the termination of a word than to its commencement, or than we do to the termination of our words. The end of the Latin word established that relation of the word with other words which we establish by prepositions or auxiliary verbs. Therefore, it would seem infinitely less odd to them than it does to us, to dwell at any time, for any slight purpose, abnormally, on a terminating syllable. In verse, this license – scarcely a license – would be frequently admitted. These ideas unlock the secret of such lines as the

Litoreis ingens inventa sub ilici*bus sus,*

and the

Parturiunt montes et nascitur ridicu*lus mus,*

which I quoted, some time ago, while speaking of rhyme.

As regards the prosodial elisions, such as that of *rem* before *O*, in *pulverem Olympicum*, it is really difficult to understand how so dismally silly a notion could have entered the brain even of a pedant. Were it demanded of me why the books cut off one *vowel* before another, I might say – it is, perhaps, because the books think that, since a bad reader is so apt to slide the one vowel into the other at any rate, it is just as well to print them *ready-slided*. But in the case of the terminating *m*, which is the most readily pronounced of all consonants, (as the infantile *mama* will testify,) and the most impossible to cheat the ear of by any system of sliding – in the case of the *m*, I should be driven to reply that, to the

133

best of my belief, the prosodists did the thing, because they had a fancy for doing it, and wished to see how funny it would look after it was done. The thinking reader will perceive that, from the great facility with which *em* may be enunciated, it is admirably suited to form one of the rapid short syllables in the bastard dactyl (pulverem O); but because the books had no conception of a bastard dactyl, they knocked it in the head at once – by cutting off its tail!

Let me now give a specimen of the true scansion of another Horatian measure; embodying an instance of proper elision.

> Integer | vitæ | scelerisque | purus |
> Non eget | Mauri | jaculis ne | que arcu |
> Nec vene | natis | gravida sa | gittis,
>   Fusce, pha | retrâ.

Here the regular recurrence of the bastard dactyl, gives great animation to the rhythm. The *e* before the *a* in *que arcu*, is, almost of sheer necessity, cut off – that is to say, run into the *a* so as to preserve the spondee. But even this license it would have been better not to take.

Had I space, nothing would afford me greater pleasure than to proceed with the scansion of *all* the ancient rhythms, and to show how easily, by the help of common sense, the intended music of each and all can be rendered instantaneously apparent. But I have already overstepped my limits, and must bring this paper to an end.

It will never do, however, to omit all mention of the heroic hexameter.

I began the 'processes' by a suggestion of the spondee as the first step towards verse. But the innate monotony of the spondee has caused its disappearance, as the basis of rhythm, from all modern poetry. We *may* say, indeed, that the French heroic – the most wretchedly monotonous verse in existence – is, to all intents and purposes, spondaic. But it is not designedly spondaic – and if the French were ever to examine it at all, they would no doubt pronounce it iambic. It must be observed, that the French language is strangely peculiar in this point – *that it is without accentuation and consequently without verse.* The genius of the people, rather than the structure of the tongue, declares that their words are, for the most part, enunciated with an uniform dwelling on each syllable. For example – *we* say, 'syl*la*bification'. A Frenchman would say, syl-la-bi-fi-ca-ti-on; dwelling on no one of the syllables with any noticeable particularity. Here again I put an extreme case, in order to be well understood; but the general fact is as I give it – that, comparatively, the French have *no* accentuation. And there can be nothing worth the name of verse, without. Therefore, the French have no verse worth the name – which is the fact, put in sufficiently plain terms. Their iambic rhythm so superabounds in absolute spondees as to warrant me in calling its basis spondaic; but French is the *only* modern tongue which has any rhythm with such basis; and even in the French, it is, as I have said, unintentional.

Admitting, however, the validity of my suggestion, that the spondee was the first approach to verse, we should expect to find, first, natural spondees (words each forming just a spondee,) most abundant in the most ancient languages; and, secondly, we should expect to find spondees forming the basis of the most ancient rhythms. These expectations are in both cases confirmed.

Of the Greek hexameter, the intentional basis is spondaic. The dactyls are the *variation* of the theme. It will be observed that there is no absolute certainty about *their* points of interposition. The penultimate foot, it is true, is usually a dactyl; but not uniformly so; while the ultimate, on which the ear *lingers* is always a spondee. Even that the penultimate is usually a dactyl may be clearly referred to the necessity of winding up with the *distinctive* spondee. In corroboration of this idea, again, we should look to find the penultimate spondee most usual in the most ancient verse; and, accordingly, we find it more frequent in the Greek than in the Latin hexameter.

But besides all this, spondees are not only more prevalent in the heroic hexameter than dactyls, but occur to such an extent as is even unpleasant to modern ears, on account of monotony. What the modern chiefly appreciates and admires in the Greek hexameter, is the *melody of the abundant vowel sounds*. The Latin

135

hexameters *really* please very few moderns – although so many pretend to fall into ecstasies about them. In the hexameters quoted, several pages ago, from Silius Italicus, the preponderance of the spondee is strikingly manifest. Besides the natural spondees of the Greek and Latin, numerous artificial ones arise in the verse of these tongues on account of the tendency which *case* has to throw full accentuation on terminal syllables; and the preponderance of the spondee is farther ensured by the comparative infrequency of the small prepositions which *we* have to serve us *instead* of case, and also the absence of the diminutive auxiliary verbs with which *we* have to eke out the expression of our primary ones. These are the monosyllables whose abundance serve to stamp the poetic genius of a language as tripping or dactylic.

Now paying no attention to these facts, Sir Philip Sidney, Professor Longfellow, and innumerable other persons more or less modern, have busied themselves in constructing what they supposed to be 'English hexameters on the model of the Greek'. The only difficulty was that (even leaving out of question the melodious masses of vowel,) these gentlemen never could get their English hexameters to *sound* Greek. Did they *look* Greek? – that should have been the query; and the reply might have led to a solution of the riddle. In placing a copy of ancient hexameters side by side with a copy (in similar type) of such hexameters as Professor Longfellow, or Professor Felton, or the Frogpondian Professors collectively, are in the shameful practice of composing 'on the model of the Greek', it will be seen that the latter (hexameters, not professors) are about one third longer *to the eye*, on an average, than the former. The more abundant dactyls make the difference. And it is the greater number of spondees in the Greek than in the English – in the ancient than in the modern tongue – which has caused it to fall out that while these eminent scholars were groping about in the dark for a Greek hexameter, which is a spondaic rhythm varied now and then by dactyls, they merely stumbled, to the lasting scandal of scholarship, over something which, on account of its long-leggedness, we may as well term a Feltonian hexameter, and which is a dactylic rhythm, interrupted, rarely, by artificial spondees which are no spondees at all, and which are curiously thrown in by the heels at all kinds of improper and impertinent points.

Here is a specimen of the Longfellownian hexameter,

Also the | church with | in was a | dorned for | this was the | season |
In which the | young their | parents' | hope and the | loved ones of | Heaven |
Should at the | foot of the | altar re | new the | vows of their | baptism |
Therefore each | nook and | corner was | swept and | cleaned and the | dust was |
Blown from the | walls and | ceiling and | from the | oil-painted | benches. |

Mr Longfellow is a man of imagination – but *can* he imagine that any individual, with a proper understanding of the danger of lockjaw, would make the attempt of twisting his mouth into the shape necessary for the emission of such spondees as 'par*ents*', or such dactyls as 'cleaned and the' and 'loved ones of'? 'Baptism' is by no means a bad spondee – perhaps because it happens to be a dactyl; – of all the rest, however, I am dreadfully ashamed.

But these feet – dactyls and spondees, all together, – should thus be put at once into their proper position:

Also, the church within was adorned; for this was the season in which the young, their parents' hope, and the loved ones of Heaven, should, at the feet of the altar, renew the vows of their baptism. Therefore, each nook and corner was swept and cleaned; and the dust was blown from the walls and ceiling, and from the oil-painted benches.

There! – that is respectable prose; and it will incur no danger of ever getting its character ruined by any body's mistaking it for verse.

But even when we let these modern hexameters go, as Greek, and merely hold them fast in their proper character of Longfellownian, or Feltonian, or Frogpondian, we must still condemn them as having been committed in a radical misconception of the philosophy of verse. The spondee, as I observed, is the *theme* of

137

the Greek line. Most of the ancient hexameters *begin* with spondees, for the reason that the spondee *is* the theme; and the ear is filled with it as with a burden. Now the Feltonian dactylics have, in the same way, dactyls for the theme, and most of them begin with dactyls – which is all very proper if not very Greek – but, unhappily, the one point at which they *are* very Greek is that point, precisely, at which they should be nothing but Feltonian. They always *close* with what is meant for a spondee. To be consistently silly, they should die off in a dactyl.

That a truly Greek hexameter *cannot*, however, be readily composed in English, is a proposition which I am by nomeans inclined to admit. I think I could manage the point myself. For example:

Do tell! | when may we | hope to make | men of sense | out of
    the | Pundits |
Born and brought | up with their | snouts deep | down in the |
    mud of the | Frog-pond?
Why ask? | who ever | yet saw | money made | out of a | fat old |
    Jew, or | downright | upright | nutmegs | out of a | pine-
    knot? |

The proper spondee predominance is here preserved. Some of the dactyls are not so good as I could wish – but, upon the whole, the rhythm is very decent – to say nothing of its excellent sense.

The Philosophy of Composition

Charles Dickens, in a note now lying before me, alluding to an examination I once made of the mechanism of *Barnaby Rudge*, says – 'By the way, are you aware that Godwin wrote his *Caleb Williams* backwards? He first involved his hero in a web of difficulties, forming the second volume, and then, for the first, cast about him for some mode of accounting for what had been done.'

I cannot think this the *precise* mode of procedure on the part of Godwin – and indeed what he himself acknowledges, is not altogether in accordance with Mr Dickens' idea – but the author of *Caleb Williams* was too good an artist not to perceive the advantage derivable from at least a somewhat similar process. Nothing is more clear than that every plot, worth the name, must be elaborated to its *dénouement* before anything be attempted with the pen. It is only with the *dénouement* constantly in view that we can give a plot its indispensable air of consequence, or causation, by making the incidents, and especially the tone at all points, tend to the development of the intention.

There is a radical error, I think, in the usual mode of constructing a story. Either history affords a thesis – or one is suggested by an incident of the day – or, at best, the author sets himself to work in the combination of striking events to form merely the basis of his narrative – designing, generally, to fill in with description, dialogue, or autorial comment, whatever crevices of fact, or action, may, from page to page, render themselves apparent.

I prefer commencing with the consideration of an *effect*. Keeping originality *always* in view – for he is false to himself who ventures to dispense with so obvious and so easily attainable a source of interest – I say to myself, in the first place, 'Of the innumerable effects, or impressions, of which the heart, the intellect, or (more generally) the soul is susceptible, what one shall I, on the present occasion, select?' Having chosen a novel, first, and secondly a vivid effect, I consider whether it can be best wrought by incident or tone – whether by ordinary incidents and peculiar tone, or the converse, or by peculiarity both of incident and tone – afterward looking about me (or rather within) for such combinations of event, or tone, as shall best aid me in the construction of the effect.

I have often thought how interesting a magazine paper might be written by any author who would – that is to say who could – detail, step by step, the processes by which any one of his compositions attained its ultimate point of completion. Why such a paper has never been given to the world, I am much at a loss to say – but, perhaps, the autorial vanity has had more to do with the omission than any one other cause. Most writers – poets in especial – prefer having it understood that they compose by a species of fine frenzy – an ecstatic intuition – and would positively shudder at letting the public take a peep behind the scenes, at the elaborate and vacillating crudities of thought – at the true purposes seized only at the last moment – at the innumerable glimpses of idea that arrived not at the maturity of full view – at the fully matured fancies discarded in despair as unmanageable – at the cautious selections and rejections – at the painful erasures and interpolations – in a word, at the wheels and pinions – the tackle for scene-shifting – the step-ladders and demon-traps – the cock's feathers, the red paint and the black patches, which, in ninety-nine cases out of the hundred, constitute the properties of the literary *histrio*.

I am aware, on the other hand, that the case is by no means common, in which an author is at all in condition to retrace the steps by which his conclusions have been attained. In general, suggestions, having arisen pell-mell, are pursued and forgotten in a similar manner.

For my own part, I have neither sympathy with the repugnance alluded to, nor, at any time the least difficulty in recalling to mind the progressive steps of any of my compositions; and, since the interest of an analysis, or reconstruction, such as I have considered a *desideratum*, is quite independent of any real or fancied interest in the thing analyzed, it will not be regarded as a breach of decorum on my part to show the *modus operandi* by which some one of my own works was put together. I select 'The Raven', as most generally known. It is my design to render it manifest that no one point in its composition is referable either to accident or intuition – that the work proceeded, step by step, to its completion with the precision and rigid consequence of a mathematical problem.

Let us dismiss, as irrelevant to the poem, *per se*, the circumstance – or say the necessity – which, in the first place, gave rise to the intention of composing a poem that should suit at once the popular and the critical taste.

We commence, then, with this intention.

The initial consideration was that of extent. If any literary work is too long to be read at one sitting, we must be content to dispense with the immensely important effect derivable from unity of impression – for, if two sittings be required, the affairs of the world interfere, and every thing like totality is at once destroyed. But since, *ceteris paribus*, no poet can afford to dispense with *any thing* that may advance his design, it but remains to be seen whether there is, in extent, any advantage to counterbalance the loss of unity which attends it. Here I say no, at once. What we term a long poem is, in fact, merely a succession of brief ones – that is to say, of brief poetical effects. It is needless to demonstrate that a poem is such, only inasmuch as it intensely excites, by elevating, the soul; and all intense excitements are, through a psychal necessity, brief. For this reason, at least one half of the *Paradise Lost* is essentially prose – a succession of poetical excitements interspersed, *inevitably*, with corresponding depressions – the whole being deprived, through the extremeness of its length, of the vastly important artistic element, totality, or unity, of effect.

It appears evident, then, that there is a distinct limit, as regards length, to all works of literary art – the limit of a single sitting – and that, although in certain classes of prose composition, such as *Robinson Crusoe*, (demanding no unity,) this limit may be advantageously overpassed, it can never properly be overpassed in a poem. Within this limit, the extent of a poem may be made to bear mathematical relation to its merit – in other words, to the excitement or elevation which it is capable of inducing; for it is clear that the brevity must be in direct ratio of the intensity of the intended effect: – this, with one proviso – that a certain degree of duration is absolutely requisite for the production of any effect at all.

Holding in view these considerations, as well as that degree of excitement which I deemed not above the popular, while not below the critical, taste, I reached at once what I conceived the proper *length* for my intended poem – a length of about one hundred lines. It is, in fact, a hundred and eight.

My next thought concerned the choice of an impression, or effect, to be conveyed: and here I may as well observe that, throughout the construction, I kept steadily in view the design of rendering the work *universally* appreciable. I should be carried too far out of my immediate topic were I to demonstrate a point upon which I have repeatedly insisted, and which, with the poetical, stands not in the slightest need of demonstration – the point, I mean, that Beauty is the sole legitimate province of the poem. A few words, however, in elucidation of my real meaning, which some of my friends have evinced a disposition to misrepresent. That pleasure which is at once the most intense, the most elevating, and the most pure, is, I believe, found in the contemplation of the beautiful. When, indeed, men speak of Beauty, they mean, precisely, not a quality, as is supposed, but an effect – they refer, in short, just to that intense and pure elevation of *soul – not* of intellect, or of heart – upon which I have commented, and which is experienced in consequence of contemplating 'the beautiful'. Now I designate Beauty as the province of the poem, merely because it is an obvious rule of Art that effects should be made to spring from direct causes – that objects should be attained through means best adapted for their attainment – no one as yet having been weak enough to deny that the peculiar elevation alluded to is *most readily* attained in the poem. Now the object, Truth, or the satisfaction of the intellect, and the object Passion, or the excitement of the heart, are, although attainable, to a certain extent, in poetry, far more readily attainable in prose. Truth, in fact, demands a precision, and Passion a *homeliness* (the truly passionate will comprehend me) which are absolutely antagonistic to that Beauty which, I maintain, is the excitement, or pleasureable elevation, of the soul. It by no means follows from any thing here said, that passion, or even truth, may not be introduced, and even profitably introduced, into a poem – for they may serve in elucidation, or aid the general effect, as do discords in music, by contrast – but the true artist will always contrive, first, to tone them into proper subservience to the predominant aim, and, secondly, to enveil them, as far as possible, in that Beauty which is the atmosphere and the essence of the poem.

Regarding, then, Beauty as my province, my next question referred to the *tone* of its highest manifestation – and all experience has shown that this tone is one of *sadness*. Beauty of whatever kind, in its supreme development, invariably excites the sensitive soul to tears. Melancholy is thus the most legitimate of all the poetical tones.

The length, the province, and the tone, being thus determined,

I betook myself to ordinary induction, with the view of obtaining some artistic piquancy which might serve me as a key-note in the construction of the poem – some pivot upon which the whole structure might turn. In carefully thinking over all the usual artistic effects – or more properly *points*, in the theatrical sense – I did not fail to perceive immediately that no one had been so universally employed as that of the *refrain*. The universality of its employment sufficed to assure me of its intrinsic value, and spared me the necessity of submitting it to analysis. I considered it, however, with regard to its susceptibility of improvement, and soon saw it to be in a primitive condition. As commonly used, the *refrain*, or burden, not only is limited to lyric verse, but depends for its impression upon the force of monotone – both in sound and thought. The pleasure is deduced solely from the sense of identity – of repetition. I resolved to diversify, and so heighten, the effect, by adhering, in general, to the monotone of sound, while I continually varied that of thought: that is to say, I determined to produce continuously novel effects, by the variation *of the application* of the *refrain* – the *refrain* itself remaining, for the most part, unvaried.

These points being settled, I next bethought me of the *nature* of my *refrain*. Since its application was to be repeatedly varied, it was clear that the *refrain* itself must be brief, for there would have been an insurmountable difficulty in frequent variations of application in any sentence of length. In proportion to the brevity of the sentence, would, of course, be the facility of the variation. This led me at once to a single word as the best *refrain*.

The question now arose as to the *character* of the word. Having made up my mind to a *refrain*, the division of the poem into stanzas was, of course, a corollary: the *refrain* forming the close of each stanza. That such a close, to have force, must be sonorous and susceptible of protracted emphasis, admitted no doubt: and these considerations inevitably led me to the long *o* as the most sonorous vowel, in connection with *r* as the most producible consonant.

The sound of the *refrain* being thus determined, it became necessary to select a word embodying this sound, and at the same time in the fullest possible keeping with that melancholy which I had predetermined as the tone of the poem. In such a search it would have been absolutely impossible to overlook the word 'Nevermore'. In fact, it was the very first which presented itself.

The next *desideratum* was a pretext for the continuous use of the one word 'nevermore'. In observing the difficulty which I at once found in inventing a sufficiently plausible reason for its continuous repetition, I did not fail to perceive that this difficulty arose solely from the pre-assumption that the word was to be so continuously or monotonously spoken by a *human* being – I did not fail to perceive, in short, that the difficulty lay in the reconciliation of this monotony with the exercise of reason on the part of the creature repeating the word. Here, then, immediately arose the idea of a *non*-reasoning creature capable of speech; and, very naturally, a parrot, in the first instance, suggested itself, but was superseded forthwith by a Raven, as equally capable of speech, and infinitely more in keeping with the intended *tone*.

I had now gone so far as the conception of a Raven – the bird of ill omen – monotonously repeating the one word, 'Nevermore', at the conclusion of each stanza, in a poem of melancholy tone, and in length about one hundred lines. Now, never losing sight of the object *supremeness*, or perfection, at all points, I asked myself – 'Of all melancholy topics, what, according to the *universal* understanding of mankind, is the *most* melancholy?' Death – was the obvious reply. 'And when,' I said, 'is this most melancholy of topics most poetical?' From what I have already explained at some length, the answer, here also, is obvious – 'When it most closely allies itself to *Beauty:* the death, then, of a beautiful woman is, unquestionably, the most poetical topic in the world – and equally is it beyond doubt that the lips best suited for such topic are those of a bereaved lover.'

I had now to combine the two ideas, of a lover lamenting his deceased mistress and a Raven continuously repeating the word 'Nevermore'. – I had to combine these, bearing in mind my design of varying, at every turn, the *application* of the word repeated; but the only intelligible mode of such combination is that of imagining the Raven employing the word in answer to the queries of the lover. And here it was that I saw at once the opportunity afforded

144

for the effect on which I had been depending – that is to say, the effect of the *variation of application*. I saw that I could make the first query propounded by the lover – the first query to which the Raven should reply 'Nevermore' – that I could make this first query a commonplace one – until at length the lover, startled from his original *nonchalance* by the melancholy character of the word itself – by its frequent repetition – and by a consideration of the ominous reputation of the fowl that uttered it – is at length excited to superstition, and wildly propounds queries of a far different character – queries whose solution he has passionately at heart – propounds them half in superstition and half in that species of despair which delights in self-torture – propounds them not altogether because he believes in the prophetic or demoniac character of the bird (which, reason assures him, is merely repeating a lesson learned by rote) but because he experiences a phrenzied pleasure in so modeling his questions as to receive from the *expected* 'Nevermore' the most delicious because the most intolerable of sorrow. Perceiving the opportunity thus afforded me – or, more strictly, thus forced upon me in the progress of the construction – I first established in mind the climax, or concluding query – that query to which 'Nevermore' should be in the last place an answer – that in reply to which this word 'Nevermore' should involve the utmost conceivable amount of sorrow and despair.

Here then the poem may be said to have its beginning – at the end, where all works of art should begin – for it was here, at this point of my preconsiderations, that I first put pen to paper in the composition of the stanza:

'Prophet,' said I, 'thing of evil! prophet still if bird or devil!
By that heaven that bends above us – by that God we both adore,
Tell this soul with sorrow laden, if within the distant Aidenn,
It shall clasp a sainted maiden whom the angels name Lenore –
Clasp a rare and radiant maiden whom the angels name Lenore.'
Quoth the Raven 'Nevermore.'

I composed this stanza, at this point, first that, by establishing the climax, I might the better vary and graduate, as regards seriousness and importance, the preceding queries of the lover –

145

and, secondly, that I might definitely settle the rhythm, the metre, and the length and general arrangement of the stanza – as well as graduate the stanzas which were to precede, so that none of them might surpass this in rhythmical effect. Had I been able, in the subsequent composition, to construct more vigorous stanzas, I should, without scruple, have purposely enfeebled them, so as not to interfere with the climacteric effect.

And here I may as well say a few words of the versification. My first object (as usual) was originality. The extent to which this has been neglected, in versification, is one of the most unaccountable things in the world. Admitting that there is little possibility of variety in mere *rhythm*, it is still clear that the possible varieties of metre and stanza are absolutely infinite – and yet, *for centuries, no man, in verse, has ever done, or ever seemed to think of doing, an original thing*. The fact is, that originality (unless in minds of very unusual force) is by no means a matter, as some suppose, of impulse or intuition. In general, to be found, it must be elaborately sought, and although a positive merit of the highest class, demands in its attainment less of invention than negation.

Of course, I pretend to no originality in either the rhythm or metre of the 'Raven'. The former is trochaic – the latter is octa-meter acatalectic, alternating with heptameter catalectic repeated in the *refrain* of the fifth verse, and terminating with tetrameter catalectic. Less pedantically – the feet employed throughout (trochees) consist of a long syllable followed by a short: the first line of the stanza consists of eight of these feet – the second of seven and a half (in effect two-thirds) – the third of eight – the fourth of seven and a half – the fifth the same – the sixth three and a half. Now, each of these lines, taken individually, has been employed before, and what originality the 'Raven' has, is in their *combination into stanza;* nothing even remotely approaching this combination has ever been attempted. The effect of this original-ity of combination is aided by other unusual, and some altogether novel effects, arising from an extension of the application of the principles of rhyme and alliteration.

The next point to be considered was the mode of bringing together the lover and the Raven – and the first branch of this con-sideration was the *locale*. For this the most natural suggestion might seem to be a forest, or the fields – but it has always appeared to me that a close *circumspection of space* is absolutely necessary to the effect of insulated incident: – it has the force of a frame to a picture. It has an indisputable moral power in keeping concentrated the attention, and, of course, must not be confounded with mere unity of place.

I determined then, to place the lover in his chamber – in a chamber rendered sacred to him by memories of her who had frequented it. The room is represented as richly furnished – this in mere pursuance of the ideas I have already explained on the subject of Beauty, as the sole true poetical thesis.

The *locale* being thus determined, I had now to introduce the bird – and the thought of introducing him through the window, was inevitable. The idea of making the lover suppose, in the first instance, that the flapping of the wings of the bird against the shutter, is a 'tapping' at the door, originated in a wish to increase, by prolonging, the reader's curiosity, and in a desire to admit the incidental effect arising from the lover's throwing open the door, finding all dark, and thence adopting the half-fancy that it was the spirit of his mistress that knocked.

I made the night tempestuous, first, to account for the Raven's seeking admission, and secondly, for the effect of contrast with the (physical) serenity within the chamber.

I made the bird alight on the bust of Pallas, also for the effect of contrast between the marble and the plumage – it being understood that the bust was absolutely *suggested* by the bird – the bust of *Pallas* being chosen, first, as most in keeping with the scholarship of the lover, and, secondly, for the sonorousness of the word, Pallas, itself.

About the middle of the poem, also, I have availed myself of the force of contrast, with a view of deepening the ultimate impression. For example, an air of the fantastic – approaching as nearly to the ludicrous as was admissible – is given to the Raven's entrance. He comes in 'with many a flirt and flutter'.

Not the *least obeisance made he* – not a moment stopped or
    stayed he,
But with the mien of lord or lady, perched above my chamber door.

In the two stanzas which follow, the design is more obviously carried out: –

Then this ebony bird beguiling my sad fancy into smiling
By the *grave and stern decorum of the countenance it wore*,
'Though thy *crest be shorn and shaven* thou,' I said, 'art sure no craven,
Ghastly grim and ancient Raven wandering from the nightly shore –
Tell me what thy lordly name is on the Night's Plutonian shore?'
            Quoth the Raven 'Nevermore.'

Much I marvelled *this ungainly fowl* to hear discourse so plainly
Though its answer little meaning – little relevancy bore;
For we cannot help agreeing that no living human being
Ever yet was blessed with seeing bird above his chamber door –
Bird or beast upon the sculptured bust above his chamber door,
            With such name as 'Nevermore.'

The effect of the *dénouement* being thus provided for, I immediately drop the fantastic for a tone of the most profound seriousness: – this tone commencing in the stanza directly following the one last quoted, with the line,

But the Raven, sitting lonely on that placid bust, spoke only, etc.

From this epoch the lover no longer jests – no longer sees any thing even of the fantastic in the Raven's demeanor. He speaks of him as a 'grim, ungainly, ghastly, gaunt, and ominous bird of yore,' and feels the 'fiery eyes' burning into his 'bosom's core'. This revolution of thought, or fancy, on the lover's part, is intended to induce a similar one on the part of the reader – to bring the mind into a proper frame for the *dénouement* – which is now brought about as rapidly and as *directly* as possible.

With the *dénouement* proper – with the Raven's reply, 'Nevermore', to the lover's final demand if he shall meet his mistress in another world – the poem, in its obvious phase, that of a simple narrative, may be said to have its completion. So far, every thing is within the limits of the accountable – of the real. A raven, having learned by rote the single word 'Nevermore', and having

148

escaped from the custody of its owner, is driven at midnight, through the violence of a storm, to seek admission at a window from which a light still gleams – the chamber-window of a student, occupied half in poring over a volume, half in dreaming of a beloved mistress deceased. The casement being thrown open at the fluttering of the bird's wings, the bird itself perches on the most convenient seat out of the immediate reach of the student, who, amused by the incident and the oddity of the visitor's demeanor, demands of it, in jest and without looking for a reply, its name. The raven addressed, answers with its customary word, 'Nevermore' – a word which finds immediate echo in the melancholy heart of the student, who, giving utterance aloud to certain thoughts suggested by the occasion, is again startled by the fowl's repetition of 'Nevermore'. The student now guesses the state of the case, but is impelled, as I have before explained, by the human thirst for self-torture, and in part by superstition, to propound such queries to the bird as will bring him, the lover, the most of the luxury of sorrow, through the anticipated answer 'Nevermore'. With the indulgence, to the extreme, of this self-torture, the narration, in what I have termed its first or obvious phase, has a natural termination, and so far there has been no overstepping of the limits of the real.

But in subjects so handled, however skilfully, or with however vivid an array of incident, there is always a certain hardness or nakedness, which repels the artistical eye. Two things are invariably required – first, some amount of complexity, or more properly, adaptation; and, secondly, some amount of suggestiveness – some under-current, however indefinite, of meaning. It is this latter, in especial, which imparts to a work of art so much of that *richness* (to borrow from colloquy a forcible term) which we are too fond of confounding with *the ideal*. It is the *excess* of the suggested meaning – it is the rendering this the upper instead of the under current of the theme – which turns into prose (and that of the very flattest kind) the so called poetry of the so called transcendentalists.

Holding these opinions, I added the two concluding stanzas of the poem – their suggestiveness being thus made to pervade all the narrative which has preceded them. The under-current of meaning is rendered first apparent in the lines –

'Take thy beak from out *my heart*, and take thy form from off
    my door!'
                    Quoth the Raven 'Nevermore!'

It will be observed that the words, 'from out my heart,' involve
the first metaphorical expression in the poem. They, with the
answer, 'Nevermore', dispose the mind to seek a moral in all that
has been previously narrated. The reader begins now to regard
the Raven as emblematical – but it is not until the very last line of
the very last stanza, that the intention of making him emblemati-
cal of *Mournful and Never-ending Remembrance* is permitted dis-
tinctly to be seen:

And the Raven, never flitting, still is sitting, still is sitting,
On the pallid bust of Pallas, just above my chamber door;
And his eyes have all the seeming of a demon's that is
    dreaming,
And the lamplight o'er him streaming throws his shadow on
    the floor;
And my soul *from out that shadow* that lies floating on the floor
                Shall be lifted – nevermore.